God Said What

*Answering the Hard Questions
of the Bible*

DAN VER WOERT

WESTBOW PRESS
A DIVISION OF THOMAS NELSON
& ZONDERVAN

Copyright © 2015 Dan Ver Woert.

All rights reserved. No part of this book may be used or reproduced by any means, graphic, electronic, or mechanical, including photocopying, recording, taping or by any information storage retrieval system without the written permission of the publisher except in the case of brief quotations embodied in critical articles and reviews.

Scripture taken from the Holy Bible, NEW INTERNATIONAL VERSION®. Copyright © 1973, 1978, 1984 by Biblica, Inc. All rights reserved worldwide. Used by permission. NEW INTERNATIONAL VERSION® and NIV® are registered trademarks of Biblica, Inc. Use of either trademark for the offering of goods or services requires the prior written consent of Biblica US, Inc.

WestBow Press books may be ordered through booksellers or by contacting:

WestBow Press
A Division of Thomas Nelson & Zondervan
1663 Liberty Drive
Bloomington, IN 47403
www.westbowpress.com
1 (866) 928-1240

Because of the dynamic nature of the Internet, any web addresses or links contained in this book may have changed since publication and may no longer be valid. The views expressed in this work are solely those of the author and do not necessarily reflect the views of the publisher, and the publisher hereby disclaims any responsibility for them.

Any people depicted in stock imagery provided by Thinkstock are models, and such images are being used for illustrative purposes only. Certain stock imagery © Thinkstock.

ISBN: 978-1-4908-7739-6 (sc)
ISBN: 978-1-4908-7740-2 (hc)
ISBN: 978-1-4908-7738-9 (e)

Library of Congress Control Number: 2015906183

Print information available on the last page.

WestBow Press rev. date: 04/22/2015

Contents

Introduction: Dan's Personal Disclaimer vii

1. Why was a man stoned for collecting firewood on the Sabbath?....... 1
2. Why did God command bears to maul teenagers? 5
3. Why did God say, "When you take the city, kill every man woman, and child"? 9
4. Did God condone slavery? 19
5. Why was God's judgment on sin so severe at times? 27
6. Why does God call homosexuality an abomination? 35
7. Did Jesus ever address the subject of homosexuality? 41
8. Did Jesus ever address the issue of how to deal with a pedophile or someone who has bizarre sexual urges? 45
9. Why did God order the execution of anyone who cursed his mother and father? 49
10. Did God say, If a man rapes a woman, he has to marry her? 53
11. Why Did God command us to take our dead brother's spouse as a wife? 57
12. Why did God condemn a man for not impregnating his dead brother's wife? 61
13. Why did God strike a man dead for touching the ark of the covenant? 67
14. Is suicide the unpardonable sin? 71
15. Would Jesus have supported the death penalty? 81
16. Is it permissible for a woman to speak in church? 85

Conclusion: Where do we go from here? 93

Introduction

Dan's Personal Disclaimer

Usually when someone writes a book about the Bible, there's a foreword by someone way more important than the author, a preface by someone a whole lot smarter, and then an introduction by someone seemingly a lot more spiritual. Well, I don't have a lot of influential friends; instead, I'm just going to write my own personal disclaimer.

I'm inviting you to take a spiritual journey with me because the real purpose of this book is to start a dialogue between skeptics and believers—a conversation that's way overdue. At the age of twenty-one, I had my first real "God encounter," and I sat down to read the Bible for the first time. I wrestled to understand things that made me frequently go, "What?" Thus the title: *God Said What?* This book is a result of that spiritual pilgrimage. It's the book I wish someone had given to me my first day of Bible college or my first day in ministry.

I asked my pastor to explain these things to me, and I got an elusive answer. In Bible college, every professor gave me even better elusive answer. Not that their answers were intentionally bad; I just never got answers I was okay with—answers that made sense or that settled the issues in my heart.

I asked one of my professors privately, "Okay, Bigfoot, the Loch Ness monster, flying saucers, and the Devil's triangle, how do you explain all that from a biblical perspective?"

His answer: "Even if I could answer all of those questions, the answers would not be edifying, and that is why God has not allowed us to understand those things."

Let's never forget that God's silence on an issue does not equal indifference.

I'm not a Bible scholar. I'm a Christian philosopher. I set a stage complete with a cast and background characters into a particular scene. Then I impose a hypothetical what-if scenario into the script. If this is what was going on in the background when God commanded Moses to do a certain thing, his thinking was rational and just. If not, we're back to the drawing board, and I'm okay with that.

I know God left some mystery in the Bible for a reason, and it's to keep us on the journey. When the journey stops, the growth stops. The hardest part of this book is that I know I am trying to prove the un-provable. I was not there four thousand years ago, so I can only speculate. Just like King Solomon, I got on my knees and prayed, "Give your servant a discerning heart to govern your people, and to distinguish between right and wrong" (1 Kings 3:9).

I love Charles Spurgeon's favorite verse, Deuteronomy 29:29.

> The secret things belong to the Lord our God." It's all about the journey and what happens on the journey really settles the issue of who I am to God and who God is to me.

I don't quote a lot of sources, and there's a reason for that. This book is not about information; it's about revelation. It's about sensing God's heart as you read the text and ask, What had to be going through his mind to make him say that?

Again, I asked God for wisdom, and in the words of John the Baptist, "A man can receive nothing unless it has been given him from heaven" (John 3:27 NASB). This book is a collection of all the little things I have picked up over the years, one small piece at a time. I have tried to file them mentally, a process of connecting the dots: reconstructing the life of an average Jewish man in 4000 BC, learning to think like an ancient Jew, and seeing the text through his eyes, as well as through the eyes of a prophet, a warrior, or a heathen king.

After reading everything I could concerning the questions in this book, I have to confess that my primary source is my own sense of spiritual intuition, answers that make sense to me. I'm resolved in them. I have peace about them. The dots all connect, and the answers seem to gel with the totality of Scripture. I even scoured the Internet and found very little. I got the impression that nobody wanted to be the guy who was wrong. So, we look the other way and just hope nobody asks, right?

If I were to cite one primary source, it would be a book I read my second year of Bible college, when I was asked to be in an Honors Seminar at North Central University with Dr. Gordon Anderson. He had me read *The Institutes of Biblical Law* by R. J. Rushdoony. It got me thinking in a new direction; does the law of Moses fit into my world today? It answered a few questions but not the ones I was really asking.

To anyone who has ever embraced the teachings of Jesus and the prophets, we are all painfully aware of a few "hard statements" in the Bible that have set believers against nonbelievers for way too long.

I'm glad we have this opportunity to look into God's Word together, to hear his voice, and to discern his heart. Only in those moments do we begin to see how reasonable God is and how unreasonable we are.

Writing this book was not an event but a personal crusade for truth, a collection of sound bites I have brought to the pulpit for the last twenty-five years. What really pushed me over the edge to start were several Facebook postings that asked things like "How does a loving God endorse slavery, infanticide, murder, genocide, rape, and human sacrifices?"

He doesn't. Those are all misreads on the text. These are the issues that skeptics and atheists use to discredit the teachings of the Bible. It's time we give them an answer that makes sense to them, not just to us.

One simple warning. Do not spend so much time reading books about the Bible that you forget to read the best of all books.

This book was designed to be read with your Bible in the other hand. So grab your Bible, a highlighter, and a pen, and be like the Bereans of old, who "searched the Scriptures daily to find out whether these things were so" (Acts 17:11 NKJV).

Something to ponder. There are times when the Bible simply records what happened.

Interesting fact. The Bible does not say that God told David to go kill Goliath. David stood there and heard him mock the armies of the living God and decided to shut his mouth. God may have put the idea in David's heart to throw the first punch, but it does not say that God told him to do it. It says, "This is what happened." Do I think David missed God? No? I can't answer for what someone else did three thousand years ago. I can only do what's right today.

If you find yourself not agreeing with everything in this book, that's okay. Dig deeper, and ask God for wisdom. Wrestle it through, and be honest about your convictions. I didn't write this book to see how many people I could get to agree with me. I wrote it to get everyone talking about these issues in a fresh new way. I have taken the sixteen hardest things in the Bible to explain and tried to explain them in laymen's terms.

Remember, God has called every believer to be an apologist to his generation. If you say you know who God is, people are going to ask you questions. It's your responsibility to give them biblical answers instead of cheap answers. The church needs to do better than, "Well, ya know, brother, all I can say is that God's in control." The reason you picked up this book is because God is calling you to do better than that.

The apostle Peter told us to "always be prepared to give an answer to everyone who asks you to give the reason for the hope that you have." My goal in writing this book is to raise up a generation of apologists who will not cower in the face of opposition but boldly speak the truth in love. Let's team up together!

And watch out for the naysayers. When others do not have enough intellectual gas to create their own substance, they always become professional critics. You don't need those people. They're destructive. Jesus said, "The words I have spoken to you—they are full of the Spirit and life" (John 6:63). Choose life. So, let's take a spiritual journey together.

Pastor Dan Ver Woert,

PS: After you finish this book, if it has been a blessing to you, please do not keep it a secret. Give a copy to your pastor, your Sunday school teacher, and that skeptic in your life who is so desperate to discredit the teachings of the Bible. Ask the person for feedback, and try to create a dialogue. Ask, "Would you like to take a spiritual journey together?" I wish you the best, my friend.

1

The Firewood Incident

Why was a man stoned for collecting firewood on the Sabbath?

> While the Israelites were in the wilderness, a man was found gathering wood on the Sabbath day. Those who found him gathering wood brought him to Moses and Aaron and the whole assembly, and they kept him in custody, because it was not clear what should be done to him. Then the Lord said to Moses, "The man must die. The whole assembly must stone him outside the camp." So the assembly took him outside the camp and stoned him to death, as the Lord commanded Moses. (Numbers 15:32–36)

"The man must die" (v. 35b). Oh my!

You're reading through the Bible, and you stumble across something you just can't swallow. *I get the general idea, but that's way too intense.* But just because you don't get it does not mean the answer isn't there. It just means you haven't seen it yet.

Don't ever question that God is always just or think that he is never going to over-punish someone for what he or she did contrary to his command. Remember, it was God who said, "eye for eye, tooth for tooth, hand for hand, foot for foot". (Exodus 21:24) Let the punishment fit, or be equal to, the crime. This command was never a loophole for revenge.

And remember when you read the Bible that everything is within context. Did God say that to a widow or a warrior? Did he say that to an old man or a young woman? Did he say that to a prophet or a pagan? Was that statement a universal law for an entire nation, or was he trying to teach someone a personal, private lesson? Was this a first warning or a second? Does God treat an honest mistake the same way he treats an act of willful defiance? It's all about the context.

So what do you think? Some guy is out gathering firewood on the Sabbath, and God says to take him out and stone him. Seems a little over the top, don't you think? Believe it or not, there is a very simple explanation for this.

Let's go back to Numbers 15 and read the preceding nine verses to this story, paying special attention to the words *intentional* and *unintentional*.

> Now if you *unintentionally* fail to keep any of these commands the Lord gave Moses—any of the Lord's commands to you through him, from the day the Lord gave them and continuing through the generations to come—and if this is done *unintentionally* without the community being aware of it, then the whole community is to offer a young bull for a burnt offering as an aroma pleasing to the Lord, along with its prescribed grain offering and drink offering, and a male goat for a sin offering. The priest is to make atonement for the whole Israelite community, and they will be forgiven, for it was *not intentional* and they have brought to the Lord for their wrong an offering made by fire and a sin offering. The

> whole Israelite community and the aliens living among them will be forgiven, because all the people were involved in the *unintentional* wrong. "But if just one person sins *unintentionally*, he must bring a year-old female goat for a sin offering. The priest is to make atonement before the Lord for the one who erred by sinning *unintentionally*, and when atonement has been made for him, he will be forgiven. One and the same law applies to everyone who sins *unintentionally*, whether he is a native-born Israelite or an alien. (Numbers 15:22–29, emphases added)

Did you catch that? In the preceding nine verses, God uses the word *unintentional* seven times.

So what was the context of this firewood incident? God is setting the stage and saying that this was an intentional sin, not an accident. This man stood in total defiance to the commands God had just given his chosen people. "I'm gonna do whatever I wanna do! Rules don't apply to me, not even God's rules." Arrogance. Total defiance!

Drop down in the same chapter to verses 30–31.

> But anyone who sins *defiantly*, whether native-born or alien, blasphemes the Lord, and that person must be *cut off* from his people. Because he has despised the Lord's word and broken his commands, that person must surely be *cut off*; his guilt remains on him. (emphasis added)

Did you catch that? If anyone sins *defiantly* (consciously, willingly, intentionally), this person is to be cut off and his guilt remains on him.

If you go back five chapters to Numbers 10, the children of Israel had just left Mount Sinai after seeing the fire of God rain down on the mountain. And even though God had given Moses 613 laws, he broke them down to ten very simple commands. The fourth commandment was "Remember the Sabbath day by keeping it holy." Even a man's donkey was not supposed to work on the Sabbath. This commandment was not just some indiscriminate idea that God threw out there. This was one of the Big Ten etched into a stone tablet by the finger of Yahweh.

God did not punish this man for an honest mistake but for an act of willful defiance.

This man had had fair warning, yet he chose his own way. God would never drop the hammer on someone for an unintentional mistake. You may have to live with the consequences of an unintentional mistake, but that is not the wrath of God. That is the law of sowing and reaping. In Exodus 35, God told the Israelites to pick up enough firewood on Friday to last them for two whole days. He told them to not cook from Friday evening until Saturday evening: "Prepare all your food the day before." Everyone knew this. This man's behavior was not an unintentional mistake. This was an act of willful defiance.

Did this man have previous warnings from the village elders? Was he trying to pull other people into rebellion with him? It's hard to say. But I have to believe that his conspiracy to start a rebellion was part of his punishment. Oh, and speaking of unintentional crimes, the city of refuge was not a prison. It was a safe haven a man could flee to if he committed an *unintentional* crime. That is how God views unintentional sin.

2

The Bear Mauling

Why did God command bears to maul teenagers?

Watch for the phrase, "Go on up."

> From there Elisha went up to Bethel. As he was walking along the road, some youths came out of the town and jeered at him. "*Go on up*, you baldhead!" they said. "*Go on up*, you baldhead!" He turned around, looked at them and called down a curse on them in the name of the Lord. Then two bears came out of the woods and mauled forty-two of the youths. (2 Kings 2:23–24, emphasis added)

They taunted him to "Go on up!" So do you remember what preceded this story? Elijah, Elisha's mentor and predecessor, was taken up into heaven in a whirlwind by fiery chariots and all.

That's why these young men stood there and hollered, "Go on up! Go on up!" They wanted Elisha to "go on up" in a whirlwind like Elijah did. They were not only mocking a prophet of God; they were mocking the power of the Holy Spirit. Jesus said, "I tell you the truth; all the sins and blasphemies of men will be forgiven them. But whoever blasphemes against the Holy Spirit will never be forgiven; he is guilty of an eternal sin" (Mark 3:28–29). Tough words, I know.

Making fun of a prophet's baldhead was not the mockery that inflamed God's anger. It was the mockery of the Holy Spirit that pushed him over the edge. Blasphemy of the Holy Spirit is attributing the power of God to the power of the Devil. It's calling God a counterfeit and taking his power lightly, not holding to it reverently.

The Hebrew word used is not *children* but *youths*. And it does not say that these bears killed these young men; it says that they mauled them.

The Hebrew word for *maul*, literally translated, means "to tear." Their bodies or their clothes?

Do you see someone getting a trip to the woodshed here, or does that sound a little too intense? Well, Jesus said, "It would be better for you to go through life *maimed*, that too have your entire body cast in outer darkness."

If you had to choose a trip to the woodshed now or an eternity in hell, which would you take? I'd take the bear-cub whipping any day. And maybe it was this trip to the woodshed that kept these young men from the fires of eternal punishment. How's that for a divine perspective?

It doesn't say that these two bears mauled every single person; it says they mauled forty-two of them. This must have been a very large group of adolescents; I see a real mob mentality here. One hundred teenagers against one man. Punks! I see a lone, vulnerable old man, afraid for his life and totally defenseless. The Bible tells us to honor the man of God and to respect our elders. I wouldn't be too quick to feel sorry for these renegades. I know enough about the heart of God to know that whatever they got they had coming.

Questions: Do you ever wonder if this was a turning point in someone's life? Perhaps a Damascus Road experience like the apostle Paul's? Do you ever wonder if any of these young men were later called into Elisha's School of the Prophets? I do.

3

Why did God say, "When you take the city, kill every man woman, and child"?

Samuel said to Saul, "I am the one the Lord sent to anoint you king over his people Israel; so listen now to the message from the Lord. This is what the Lord Almighty says: 'I will punish the Amalekites for what they did to Israel when they *waylaid them as they came up from Egypt*. Now go, attack the Amalekites and totally destroy all that belongs to them. Do not spare them; put to death *men and women, children and infants, cattle and sheep, camels and donkeys.*'" (1 Samuel 15:1–3, emphasis added)

That's tough to read isn't it? Before we go any farther, let's remember what God said to the prophet Ezekiel, "As I live, says the Lord God, I have no **pleasure** in the death of the wicked, but that the wicked turn from his way and live" (Ezekiel 33:11). That's where God's heart is.

But the first answer to this issue is at the end of verse 2. This was the Amalekite's punishment for what they had done to Israel when they came out of Egypt. The Amalekites ambushed them, *waylaid* them just because they were vulnerable.

When Israel came out of Egypt it was defenseless—not trained for battle and not equipped or ready to fight a war.

The Amalekites knew this and took advantage of it. God said, "eye for eye, tooth for tooth, hand for hand, foot for foot." (Exodus 21:24) Let the punishment be equal to the crime. That's the first answer.

But why didn't God just kill the men who attacked them? Why did the women and children have to die? Because in this culture, without the men to provide for and protect them, they would have died a very slow and painful death.

The women would have been raped, and the children would have been exploited in every imaginable way. Their deaths would have been slow and agonizing. This is why the prophet Jeremiah says, "Those killed by the sword are better off than those who die of famine; racked with hunger, they waste away for lack of food from the field" (Lamentations 4:9).

To kill the men and leave the women and children to fend for themselves would have been cruel. God was right when he said, "I, the Lord your God, am a jealous God, visiting the iniquity of the fathers on the children, on the third and the fourth generations of those who hate Me" (Exodus 20:5). The Amalekites had brought this upon themselves. If you have a choice between a slow agonizing death and a swift one, what would you chose?

My second answer comes from our understanding of ancient history. The Assyrians, Babylonians, and Amalekites were all part of a common ancestry that inhabited the land of Canaan. Cutting off noses, ears, thumbs, and big toes was common. The Philistines gouged out Samson's eyes. This had as much to do with intimidation as it did retaliation. The people who God said to eradicate were extremely cruel people. Let's never forget that.

The Amalekites were an ancient version of terrorists we call ISIS. Their goal was never to cohabitate peacefully with Israel, their goal was to wipe them off the planet. We need to accept that. God knew it was either kill or be killed. This command was about the preservation of his chosen people.

The third answer is the big answer. I'm going to spend the next few pages trying to prove this statement, stemming from my own personal study of ancient history.

> All ancient civilizations where eventually wiped out, became extinct, or where destroyed internally because they violated one of Gods Levitical Laws on spiritual boundaries, sexual boundaries, dietary laws, or laws on personal hygiene. (David Wise, "The First Book of Public Hygiene," Answers in Genesis)

https://answersingenesis.org/biology/disease/the-first-book-of-public-hygiene/ December 1, 2003

By violating one or all of these commands, the Amalekites had brought a plague or a virus into their community that the Jews had no immunity to. The adults had infected the children through no fault of their own. But God had to make a decision. Do I let the guilty unintentionally kill the innocent, or do I punish the guilty and preserve the innocent? A tough decision I'm sure. Let's look at those violations.

1. Improper disposal of a human body

"Whoever touches a human corpse will be unclean for **seven** days" (Numbers 19:11). You think that's crazy? Read on.

Dr. Ignaz Semmelweis, known as the "savior of mothers" was teaching young medical students in Vienna in the 1850s. He noticed that so many babies were dying of puerperal fever. Then he made a connection that the dying babies were being delivered by students who had been dissecting cadavers for medical research. He made all his students wash their hands with chlorinated lime solution before delivering babies, and the mortality rate dropped to below 1 percent. According to God, they should have waited seven days after dissecting cadavers to deliver a baby. God knew they had no way of disinfecting themselves. ([Imre Zoltan, MD, "Biography, Ignaz Philipp Semmelweis," *Encyclopedia Britannica*], updated July 16, 2014. Imre Zoltan was the former professor of gynecology and obstetrics at Semmelweis Medical University, Budapest, Hungary).

2. Improper disposal of human waste

Water-borne diseases occur when a civilization gets overpopulated. This is why God told the Israelites to "bury their excrement." Remember, when this command was given, not one person in the ancient world was doing that, and it made no sense at all. I can imagine the look on everybody's faces when Moses told them that. *Why? Nobody else does it!* But today it makes perfectly good sense.

> Designate a place outside the camp where you can go to relieve yourself. As part of your equipment have something to dig with, and when you relieve yourself, dig a hole and cover up your excrement. (Deuteronomy 23:12–13)

Not the most spiritual verse in the Bible is it? My first real job was working in a sewage treatment plant for six years. I even have a degree in water and wastewater analysis from a junior college. Trust me; this makes sense. Countries and civilizations that toss their refuse on the ground, cut their feet on sharp rocks, and step in everyone's waste suffer the medical consequences of not obeying the laws of God.

A lesson from today. Here's something I learned on a recent missions trip to Haiti. Remember the earthquake that hit Haiti in 2010? Right after that happened, the United Nations showed up with relief workers from Nepal, India—soldiers from the Nepal army. They brought a unique strain of cholera the native Haitians had no immunity to. And over the next few weeks, another eight thousand Haitians died from cholera—mostly women and children because they are the water carriers in this culture.

Hundreds of thousands more ended up in the hospital, and it spread to neighboring countries like the Dominican Republic, Cuba, Venezuela, and the United States. This is why God could not let Israel intermingle with the Amalekites. "Do I punish the righteous with the wicked, or do I let the righteous remove the wicked?"

3. Drinking blood in some type of heathen sacrifice

God told Moses to drain the blood out of an animal before it was consumed. "But you must not eat meat that has its lifeblood still in it" (Genesis 9:4). This is part of what the Jews refer to as kosher—food properly prepared according to the Levitical law.

> For the life of every creature is its blood: its blood is its life. Therefore I have said to the people of Israel, You shall not eat the blood of any creature, for the life of every creature is its blood. **Whoever eats it shall be cut off.** (Leviticus 17:14 emphasis added).

Why? Because now they're infected. There is also reason to believe that our ancestors scavenged the bodies of wild animals left behind from predator attacks. What does God say about that?

"You are to be my holy people. So do not eat the meat of an animal torn by wild beasts; throw it to the dogs" (Exodus 22:31). God knew.

4. Any unnatural exchange of bodily fluids

You don't have to look very far in our world to find phrases like "yellow shower" that help us understand why God said to keep it real.

Another heathen ritual was to eat part of a deceased ancestor. Heathens believed they could take ancestors with them into the afterlife. Even up to the 1950s, tribes of cannibals in Papua New Guinea would eat the brains of their dead ancestors.

Another tribe in the Southeast Asia called the Fore tribe ate the brains of its relatives. This practice, called endocannibalism, resulted in a brain infection called kuru. The symptoms were similar to mad cow disease, a chronic wasting disease of the brain. Kuru disease was responsible for wiping out entire generations of people. (http://medlineplus.gov/).

In 2 Kings 6, when a man named Ben-Hadad, the king of Aram, besieged the city of Samaria, the siege lasted so long it created a famine. When the famine reached a breaking point, "a mule's head sold for eighty shekels of silver." They were eating the brains of an unclean animal, and eighty shekels are about two pounds of silver.

The Bible clearly teaches that when a man dies, his body goes back to dust and his spirit goes into eternity. There is nothing we can do to take our ancestors with us. We can only meet them there. If you want to see your relatives in eternity, be the leader in your family and make peace with God today, my friend.

5. Crossing the God-given boundaries of human sexuality.

"If a man has sexual relations with an animal, he is to be put to death, and you must kill the animal" (Leviticus 20:15). God did not say that to put the idea in their heads for the very first time; they were doing it! If an AIDS-type virus had infected the Jewish race, the entire race could have been wiped out, and the Messiah would never have been born.

It's hard to say what the Amalekites had been doing in their spare time, but God knew. This is why God said to kill all the "cattle and sheep, camels and donkeys." God knew what they had been subjected to and what they were infected with. When the animals were not infected, God said, "Save the best ones for yourself." When Israel destroyed the Midianites in battle, God said to spare the virgins. "Now kill all the **boys** and kill every **woman** who has **slept** with a man. But save for yourselves every **girl** who has **never slept** with a man" (Numbers 31:18). God knew who was infected and who was not.

God is just: Remember what Abraham said to God concerning the destruction of Sodom and Gomorrah?

> Far be it from you to do such a thing--to kill the righteous with the wicked, treating the righteous and the wicked alike. Far be it from you! Will not the Judge of all the earth do right?" (Genesis 18:25)

Because God is a just God, he determined it was not fair for the righteous to be destroyed with the unrighteous. The Amalekites had to go.

Bible bashers insist that God was advocating genocide. No, the Koran advocates genocide: killing infidels, people who do not believe what you believe. This was all about the preservation of the righteous, not about killing someone who believes differently than you.

Lets revisit our text. Do not spare them; put to death *men and women, children and infants,* **cattle and sheep, camels and donkeys.**" (1 Samuel 15:1–3,)

6. Eating unclean foods. Why did God classify certain animals as unclean?

Only the Israelites had a list of clean and unclean animals. The land of Canaan would not have known anything about this. AIDS, Influenza, SARS, Ebola, yellow fever, rabies, and H1N1. These diseases all come from eating unclean animals, especially when they are not properly prepared. Leviticus 18:24 says, "This is how all the nations that I am going to drive our before you became defiled!" *The land vomited them out!* Did you catch that? They killed themselves. The land vomited them out!

AIDS comes from monkeys, and people in Africa eat them—bush meat.

SARS and most flu viruses originated in southern China. Eating unclean animals exposes people to animal viruses that are incompatible with most people's immune systems.

Influenza comes from birds and pigs that spread from Chinese workers to American workers.

Ebola came from eating bats, another unclean animal. As I write this chapter in October of 2014, an Ebola crisis is sweeping western Africa. What if the Amalekites were infected with an Ebola-type virus? God knew.

Yellow fever came from monkeys. Without my yellow fever card, I was not allowed to get off the plane in Africa. It's deadly and highly contagious.

Rabies originally came from bats. But then they infected everything else. Now you can get it from dog bites or small-animal bites. It's deadly, especially in the ancient world.

H1N1 came from pigs in Mexico. Another unclean animal.

Do you notice how many of those diseases have to do with pigs, monkeys, and bats transmitting bodily fluids from animals to humans? God knew.

Again, if you were to walk into your neighbor's house in any Amalekite village, it wasn't like Mom had a list of unclean animals or hygienic laws on her refrigerator. Only the Israelites had that list.

God's law also forbids the consumption of predatory animals like lions, bears, and wolves—animals that prey on weak or diseased animals. When you eat them, directly or indirectly, you eat a weak or diseased animal.

Carrion-eaters or scavengers (vultures, hawks, eagles, coyotes, foxes, hyenas, and komodo dragons) thrive on diseased or rotting flesh. God knew eating them would pass any diseases down the food chain.

A camel is an unclean animal by biblical standards. A camel does not sweat a lot, so its body temperature rises up to 106 degrees to compensate for the additional heat. When this happens, toxins that would normally dissipate remain inside, making it unfit for human consumption. God knew.

I was on a mission's trip to Malabo Africa in 2011, where they eat a lot of rats. It's on the menu at most restaurants. And I wonder why the average life span there is forty to forty-five years of age. A rat is an unclean animal; it's a walking disease factory. Oriental rat fleas that live on black rats created the bubonic plague that killed millions of people in Europe in 1350. This is why all kinds of shots are required before visiting a third world country.

7. **Spiritual Idolatry.** In Deuteronomy 7:3–4, God warned Israel as they entered the land of Canaan.

> Do not intermarry with them. Do not give your daughters to their sons or take their daughters for your sons, for they will turn your children away from following me to serve other gods, and the Lord's anger will burn against you and will quickly destroy you.

God knew that intermingling with the Amalekites would destroy them physically, socially, and spiritually. I trust his call.

4

Did God condone slavery?

> If a man beats his male or female slave with a rod and the slave dies as a direct result, he must be punished, but he is not to be punished if the slave gets up after a day or two, since the slave is his property. (Exodus 21:20–21)

The Bible was not written in the world we live in. To understand this text, we need to understand God's judicial system under the law of Moses.

Every prison mentioned in the Bible is in a pagan culture: Egypt, Babylon, Greece, and so on. Prison was never an idea birthed in the mind of God.

I have been involved in prison ministry for over twenty years, and it's mostly a revolving door of repeat offenders. Prison systems don't work. They are built on false premises that everyone can be fixed. If that were true, why wasn't Jesus able to fix Judas? How could a man be mentored by the King of the universe and still blow it? Because he was human; It's all about choices.

Many would cite the city of refuge as a prison.

The city of refuge was not a prison; it was a safe haven, a city that a man could flee to if he committed an unintentional crime.

Here are the biblical principles for maintaining a civil society without a prison system.

According to the law of Moses, there are four options.

1. Restitution of property and goods
2. Bond servantry—often mistaken and mistranslated in the Bible as slavery
3. Excommunication—or living in the city of refuge (Deuteronomy 19: 4–7)
4. Capital punishment—the death penalty

When someone got caught committing a crime, they started at number one and hoped they didn't end up at number four. But here we're only going to deal with numbers one and two.

The first step in resolving a crime against another person was:

1. **Restitution of property and goods.** It's just what it says it is—the full and complete restitution of property that was either stolen or damaged. Plus interest fourfold. Someone killed a guy's cow; he owed a cow. He stole a hammer; he owed a hammer. Like the sign at the antique store: "You break it; you buy it!"
2. **Bond servantry.** Let's assume a person did not have the means to make restitution. Then what? He became a bond servant. Bond servantry is what the King James translators mistranslated as slavery. It's not slavery. It's a bond servant.

Any preacher who tells you the Bible advocates the kind of slavery that spawned the American Civil War is very misinformed.

"He who kidnaps a man, whether he sells him or he is found in his possession, shall surely be put to death" (Exodus 21:16). Slavery, the kidnapping, buying, and selling of human beings was a capital punishment offense in the Old Testament.

So, what is the difference between bondservant and slave? A slave is a child or someone who is abducted against his or her will. A bondservant is someone who willingly becomes a slave because he owes a debt that he cannot pay. This Scripture is referring to a grown man who was caught terrorizing innocent people. The law came to Israel as they where wandering in the dessert living in tents, and there was no infrastructure for a prison.

How did society handle a guy like that? God's answer was bond servantry. It was a legal and moral template for keeping the offender accountable to society for what he had done. Let's go back to the statement: *You can beat the slave (bond servant) because he is your property.*

Let's go back in time four thousand years and try to live in the moment. The children of Israel made it to the Promised Land. They started to settle down. They built homes and planted fields and vineyards. God blessed the labor of their hands. They built barns to hold the excess. Life was good. The people were safe and free to worship the God who led them out of Egypt.

But then a man walked into a field at harvest time in a drunken stupor, and just for kicks, he set it on fire. He burned the barns to the ground and the fields went up in flames. The livestock died from smoke inhalation. Everything was a loss, and it was a death sentence to the owner. What would an elderly couple do in this situation?

These people had no crop insurance, no government bailouts, and no disaster relief programs to turn to. There were no soup lines or Social Security benefits to fall back on when they got old. Without having something to pass on to their kids, getting old was a slow death. Having lived in the Midwest my whole life, I have many friends who are farmers, and they only get one paycheck a year. Their whole financial world revolves around this.

After the whole thing was over, the only thing the couple could do was hire themselves out as slaves. Even worse, if the man was young, would his wife and daughters have to hire themselves out as slaves or sell their bodies to the highest bidder?

One man wrecks another man's life and that's okay? No, that's not okay. They entered into a legal agreement. You will work for me for the next seven years or until the fair market value of your debt is satisfied, whichever comes first. Slaves were only retained for seven years (see Exodus 21:2). In front of the elders of the community, they "strike hands," making it official. The deal is done. Now the bond servant goes to work and fulfills his end of the deal.

But the scene changes. Three months into the agreement, the "debtor" got lazy. He told his boss to shove it! He wasn't coming to work anymore. "You're on your own, old man. I'm walking."

The owner of the bond servant shows up an hour later with the Village Elders as a rear guard. The owner of the bond servant hollered for him to get out of bed, and then smack! The man was defiant. Smack! He was still defiant. Smack! He stumbled out of the house. I guess it's time to go to work.

Remember what God said concerning the owner of a bond servant?" "An owner who hits a male or female slave in the eye and destroys it must let the slave go free to compensate for the eye. 27 And an owner who knocks out the tooth of a male or female slave must let the slave go free to compensate for the tooth." (Exodus 21:26 & 27). He had to let the slave go free because the discipline was excessive. This is not talking about human beings who were bought and sold for profit. This is about a man who destroyed another man's life and was trying to renege on his agreement to make things right.

A Lesson from Washington, DC

Several years ago Chuck Colson gave a lecture in Washington, DC, about prison reform, and when he was done, several politicians approached him.

"Where did you get an idea like this? When someone commits a crime, they have to go back and face the people they offended and work for them personally until their debt is satisfied?" Uh, the Bible.

Back in the late 1980's the State of Minnesota started a program, where offenders had to go back and face the people they had violated. Many of them ended up becoming good friends with the people that they had previously terrorized. I saw this on the local news. Why does this work? I can only speculate, but I think what happened during the restitution time is that the criminal realized he tried to take advantage of real people.

The house he tried to rob was a lot more than just an address. It was someone's home.

He realized that he stole a lot more than someone's possessions. He stole someone's peace of mind. He stole a sense of community trust. He stole a child's ability to sleep at night. He stole things that could not be replaced. And during the restitution time, the criminal is going to realize "Gee, this is how much work it takes to pay for something like this?"

There is no easy way to say this, but some of God's laws were for the incompetent, the mentally challenged, and the emotionally disadvantaged. People who were not smart enough to make an honest living and stay out of trouble. Some bond servants willingly sold themselves to wealthy landowners, knowing they would be taken care of.

The law of bond servantry was actually legal protection from tyrants who would exploit people for life because at the end of seven years, a bond servant went free. Why does God make a man strong and resourceful? It's not so he can exploit the weak. It's so he can protect the weak. But in return, the weaker members of society take on the burden of menial tasks and do it with joy, knowing that their next meal is coming from the hand they are serving.

It's a working relationship. No one is better or worse. There are some people who just need to be under the watchful eye of someone else because they just do not have the ability to take care of themselves. It's a fact of life. Jesus said, "The poor you will always have with you."

> If any of your people Hebrew men or women—**sell themselves to you** and serve you six years, in the seventh year you must let them go free. And when you release them, **do not send them away empty-handed**. Supply them **liberally** from your flock, your threshing floor and your winepress. Give to them as the Lord your God has blessed you. (Deuteronomy 15:12–13)

See what God commanded? "Do not send them away empty-handed. Supply them **liberally** from your **flock,** your **threshing floor** and your **winepress**. Give to them as the Lord your God has blessed you." Treat them like a son or a daughter. Are you getting a different picture of all this?

And let's revisit Exodus 21:21: "But he is not to be punished if the slave gets up after a day or two, since the slave is his property." Do not read anything into the text here. Most of us would assume that a slave took a day or two to get up because he was beaten so badly he was unable to walk. If you had someone working for you for free who owed you money, would you do that? That would be like beating and injuring the ox that grinds your grain.

What if this was a disgruntled employee lying there feeling sorry for himself—acting hurt and faking an injury—all the while deciding if he wants to make a run for it? Or thinking, "If I lay here and act really hurt, I can get out of this." Could someone lie there and feel sorry for himself for a couple of days and fake an injury? You bet he could.

Remember Paul's letter to Philemon. The theme of the book is, "A plea for a runaway slave." Paul was not advocating slavery. He was telling Onesimus to go back and make it right on a commitment he made to settle his debt.

This is why Paul says in verse 18, "If he has done you any wrong or owes you anything, charge it to me." Restitution of property and goods—that's the whole book of Philemon in one sentence.

One last thing. If you're going to assume that everyone who had a bond servant working for him was a heavy-handed slave master, why do we read this?

> But if the servant declares, 'I love my master and my wife and children and do not want to go free,' then his master must take him before the judges. He shall take him to the door or the doorpost and pierce his ear with an awl. Then he will be his servant for life. (Exodus 21:5–6)

How do you get a response like that if the bond servant is being beaten and mistreated? It makes no sense.

5

Why was God's judgment on sin so severe at times?

Do you wonder if God's anger ever gets away from him? Well if it does, that makes me feel a whole lot better. In all honesty, God seems to have snapped a few times in the Bible. You know, fire comes out of heaven and everything goes up in smoke! I guess God does have a breaking point, doesn't he?

The Bible has a lot to say about God's judgment. If you could condense the entire Old Testament into one statement, it would say: "If you obey me, you will be blessed, and if you disobey me, you will be cursed." It really is that simple.

But three reoccurring patterns in Scripture concern judgment.

1. **Judgment always begins at God's house.** And there is a reason for that. We, of all people, should know better. God has given us his Word; we can't say we didn't know the rules. God has given us a conscience; we can't say we had peace about doing wrong. God has given us his Spirit; we can't say we didn't have the power to change. "It is time for judgment to begin at the house of God" (1 Peter 4:17).

2. **Right after judgment, there is always grace.** Remember the flaming sword in front of the Tree of Life. If Adam had eaten of the Tree of Life in his fallen state, his soul would have been eternally condemned.
3. **God's judgment was always a demonstration of his commitment to saving lost souls.**

Let's land on reason number three. Three times in scripture we see God's judgment being extremely severe.

1. Institution of law
2. Institution of the priesthood
3. Institution of the New Testament church

Why? Because these were all institutions by which a person's sins could be atoned for and his soul could be saved. So, what do we glean from that? That God is totally serious about saving souls. Let's look at those three examples.

1. The institution of the law

In Numbers, chapter 16, we find the story of Korah's rebellion. Korah and two other men (Dathan and Abiram) decided that Moses had overstepped his boundaries. So two hundred and fifty men, all well-known community leaders, staged a rebellion against his leadership. "Moses has gone too far, and it's our job to stop him." They confronted Moses and Aaron about this and argued that the whole assembly of Israel was holy unto the Lord and not just Moses. So Moses said, "Okay, come back tomorrow and well let God decide."

The next day Korah and his two friends showed up with their wives and children. And Moses said that those who want to live should get away from their tents. God was going to settle the thing right there and then. Here was the game plan.

Moses said, "This is how you will know that the Lord has sent me to do all these things and that it was not my idea: 29 If these men die a natural death and suffer the fate of all mankind, then the Lord has not sent me. 30 But if the Lord brings about something totally new, and the earth opens its mouth and swallows them, with everything that belongs to them, and they go down alive into the realm of the dead, then you will know that these men have treated the Lord with contempt." 31 As soon as he finished saying all this, the ground under them split apart 32 and the earth opened its mouth and swallowed them and their households, and all those associated with Korah, together with their possessions. 33 They went down alive into the realm of the dead, with everything they owned; the earth closed over them, and they perished and were gone from the community. (Numbers 16: 28-33)

How do I reconcile that with a God who says of himself that his lovingkindness is everlasting?

Why did God's anger flare up over this? Well, let's go back to my original point. This was the inauguration of a new area. The institution of the Mosaic law. The law of Moses was a moral and spiritual code of conduct that a man's sins could be atoned for and his soul would be saved. God made it very clear that he was not going to let Korah and his little band of grumblers mess this thing up. So God split the ground open, and they went down into their graves alive.

This was not a lesson on how mean-spirited or hotheaded God could get. This was a demonstration of his commitment to saving lost humanity. Don't ever fight against God's plan to save humanity.

2. **The institution of priesthood.** The deaths of Nadab and Abihu, the two sons of Aaron.

> Aaron's sons Nadab and Abihu took their censers, put fire in them and added incense; and they offered

unauthorized fire before the Lord, **contrary to his command**. So fire came out from the presence of the Lord and consumed them, and they died before the Lord. (Leviticus 10:1–2)

No one knows exactly what these two men did to evoke the Lord's anger like this. Because the Bible is not absolutely clear about what *unauthorized fire* is.

A few options:

1. The coals put on the altar were not from the brazen altar but from another source.
2. It was the wrong time of day. Sacrifices were made in the morning and evening, never in between.
3. The disrespect of simply doing it wrong.
4. They were acting as mediators between God and man under the influence of alcohol. Why? Drop down six verses and read on.

Then the Lord said to Aaron, "You and your sons are not to **drink wine or other fermented drink** whenever you go into the tent of meeting, **or you will die**. This is a lasting ordinance for the generations to come, so that you can distinguish between the holy and the common, between the unclean and the clean, and so you can teach the Israelites all the decrees the Lord has given them through Moses. (Leviticus 10: 8–11)

This is the first time in the Bible that spiritual leadership is told to abstain from alcohol. Did these two men walk into the temple and do this drunk? Probably. I think there is a simple lesson to be learned here. You cannot make light of the Lord's sacrificial system without incurring his wrath. I would never want to be caught mocking the old rugged cross or the resurrection of Jesus. These are sacred truths, and we need to treat them as sacred.

Again, judgment was so severe because this was the inauguration of a new era. The Levitical priesthood was an institution by which a man's sins could be atoned for and his soul would be saved. God was not showing us what a short fuse he had or how mean he could get. He was showing us how serious he was about saving lost souls.

3. The institution of the New Testament church

Acts 5, the story of Ananias and Sapphira? They sold a piece of land and gave the money to the church. One small problem: they lied about it. They said they had given all the money to the church, but they actually kept some of it for themselves.

The sad twist to this story was Peter made it very clear that when they sold the land, the money was totally at their disposal. They were free to do with it whatever they wanted, even keeping some of it for themselves.

But Peter says, "You have not lied unto man but unto God." I think we forget how passionate God is about the proper stewardship of his resources. When I see a pastor or an evangelist who has no boundaries on how he stewards God's money, I know I'm witnessing a man who has lost the fear of God in his heart.

True story. An evangelist visited a former pastor who was serving a prison sentence for a variety of unethical mistakes. The evangelist asked him, "At what point in your ministry did you stop loving Jesus?" The pastor responded, "I never stopped loving Jesus; I stopped fearing him."

When Peter spoke to Ananias about his sin, he did this prophetically. And it was a direct revelation of a man's sin and dishonesty before God. This is what Paul refers to as a "word of knowledge"—a supernatural revelation of truth outside the realm of human understanding (see 1 Corinthians 12:8).

Peter did not pronounce judgment upon Ananias and Sapphira, he simply stated what God had already decided to do. God is the ultimate judge; we are just messengers.

God was teaching his church a lesson. A man who was full of his Spirit could discern the spirit of truth from the spirit of error. And that's why in verse 11 we read; "Great fear seized the whole church when they heard about these events!"

Would you like go to church where the leadership was so in tune with the Holy Spirit that when you were in sin, they knew it and called you out on it? Kind of scary don't you think?

A short lesson in church history. The progression of events that led up to this act of judgment is interesting.

1. The apostles were told to wait in Jerusalem for the promise of the spirit.
2. The Holy Spirit was poured out on the day of Pentecost.
3. A lame man was healed, and the ministry of signs and wonders was given to the church.
4. Three thousand souls where added to the church on one day, the first record of mass evangelism.
5. The church was purged.

Let's translate this into the twentieth century. Do you remember the five major events in the last one hundred years of the modern Pentecostal movement?

1. At the turn of century, men like Charles Parham and William Seymour tarried endlessly for a revisitation of Pentecost in America.
2. It happened. The Holy Spirit fell in Topeka, Kansas, and Los Angeles, California. We saw the great Azusa Street Revival that drew people from all over the world.

3. The Latter Rain Movement swept North America and Canada. Miracles, signs, and wonders were alive in the church again.
4. Billy Graham, mass evangelism, and high-tech global evangelism via satellite. You didn't even have to be there for God to show up and save souls.
5. The late 1980s—Jimmy Swaggart, Jim Bakker, and too many others to mention. The spirit of Ananias and Sapphira came back to the church, and the church was purged. What began in the late 1980s was Acts 5.

It fits the pattern identically. There is a little more consistency to the judgment of God than what most people tend to see.

Again, judgment was so severe because this was the inauguration of a new era. The blood of Jesus had been poured out. The message of the cross was given to the church. And this message was a means by which a man's sins could be atoned for and his soul would be saved. God is serious about saving lost souls.

6

Why does God call homosexuality an abomination?

If you're an evangelical Christian, I'm sure you know that homosexuality is one of the defining issues of our time. I'd like to take an unconventional look at this subject and then give you my personal bottom line.

The Bible clearly calls homosexuality an abomination: "You shall not lie with a male as with a woman; it is an abomination" (Leviticus 18:22). But I need to settle something here. There are eight different Hebrew words that are translated *abomination*, and some are used interchangeably. But there is always a primary use of each word in the Bible. Lets look at a few of them just to make a point.

When God calls homosexuality an abomination, he uses the word, *toebah*. This is the same word that God uses for adultery, temple prostitution, incest, cross dressing, bestiality, and child sacrifice. The strongest word possible.

When God calls unclean foods like bugs and eels an abomination, he uses the word *sheqets*.

When God calls idolatry and sorcery an abomination, he uses the word *shiqquwts*.

When God calls three-day old meat left over from a sacrifice an abomination, he uses the word *piggul*, literally translated "foul." If you eat it, you will get food poisoning (see Leviticus 7:18).

There is a powerful lesson in knowing this. Do not let some Bible-basher tell you that eating fish without scales is also listed as an abomination in the Bible. That is *sheqets*, and yes, that is the way it's translated into English. But God uses different Hebrew words to make it clear that he does not put all of these offenses on the same level.

Watch out for potholes like Genesis 43:32. When Joseph ate his first meal with his brothers, it says this,

> They served him by himself, and them by themselves, and the Egyptians who ate with him by themselves, because the Egyptians could not eat with the Hebrews, for that is an **abomination, toebah** to the Egyptians.

A liberal theologian will cite that as an abomination—a Jew eating with an Egyptian. But the text is not telling you how God felt; it's telling you how the Egyptians felt.

But why does God call homosexuality an abomination, *toebah*? What is so bad about two people who say they love each other expressing that love sexually? Well, here is my best shot at omniscience: homosexuality is a sin against the nature and character of God. And how did I come to that conclusion? The answer is in one little statement about God's creative order in Genesis, chapter 5.

> When God created mankind, he made **them** in the likeness of God. He created them male and female and blessed them. <u>And he called **them Adam**</u> when they were created. (Genesis 5:1–2)

"And he called **them Adam**." Why did he call *them* Adam?

Because the image of God was not found in the man alone or the woman alone; the image of God was found in the mystery of two becoming one.

The word *Adam* can also mean mankind, oneness, or wholeness. If it takes a man and a woman to reflect the totality of God's image, any other combination is an improper reflection of who he is. There is something about a man and a woman that reflects the wholeness or completeness of his character. A homosexual relationship does not do that. Homosexuality is called an abomination because it's a distortion of the image of God. Do you like it when people misrepresent your core values? Neither does God.

Are all sins created equal? No, they are not. First Corinthians 8:18–20 says,

> Flee from sexual immorality. **All other sins** a person commits are outside the body, **but whoever sins sexually, sins against their own body.** Do you not know that your bodies are **temples of the Holy Spirit**, who is in you, whom you have received from God? You are not your own; you were bought at a price. Therefore honor God with your bodies.

Right there, Paul makes a clear distinction between a sin that a man commits outside of his body and a sin against the temple of the Holy Spirit. All sins are not created equal. You do not go to jail for having an evil thought, but you will go to jail for life for acting out an evil thought. We all know this.

God did not make a man and a woman for Adam and say, "Take your pick." He did not make Adam a harem of fifteen women and say, "Enjoy yourself." He made one man and one woman and said, "This is your helpmate." The original plan settles the issue; this was God's plan for sexual fulfillment.

That's my theological answer.

Is homosexuality the easy way out?

I can only speak to the men on this point. Wouldn't it be easy to have a partner who had the same sex drive that you have? Yes, that would be the easy way out. And for a lot of men, the whole process of dating is quite intimidating—the first come-on line, the first date, the first move. You know what I mean? Meet the parents, aunts, uncles, grandparents, best friends, and so on. It's terrifying!

For most men a homosexual relationship would bypass all of that. You take care of me, and I'll take care of you. No warm up time, no having to win someone's heart; just an exchange of physical pleasure and it's over. I'm afraid that for a few men, homosexuality is the easy way out.

In Job chapter 36 Job makes an interesting observation about young men. Do you think AIDS is a 21st century disease? I'm not sure why the NIV translated this the way they did, but this is what it says in verse 14: *They die in their youth, among male prostitutes of the shrines.*

This is not a theological statement, but an observation from life. And what he is describing is young male prostitutes that obviously work at some type of homosexual shrine, and they are dying at a very young age. Does this ring a bell? The unintended consequences of living a life that is in direct violation of the Laws of God.

My personal opinion on homosexual marriage.

The reason I'm against homosexual marriage is because if marriage is not between a man and a woman, then marriage is between anything and anything. Once you lose that gold standard, you have opened up the institution of marriage to be anything a person can imagine. Trust me, when this experiment is over, we will all wish we hadn't let the opposition define the issue of marriage for us.

I do not see marriage as a service that the church provides; I see it as a sacred right of passage. Marriage was an institution given to us by God, and he sets the rules.

My personal bottom line.

As a Pentecostal preacher, I have an obvious theological conviction on this subject. But I also firmly believe that God has a better plan for your life. Way better. All I can do is share with you how I approach this issue on a personal basis. I have friends who are homosexuals. I have friends on Facebook who are homosexuals. I want to be the kind of man who, if any of my homosexual friends wanted to change their lives, I'd be the first person they would come talk to—an approachable, caring person.

Mr. Fred Phelps, the infamous self-proclaimed pastor from Westboro Baptist Church, is not that man. He's a total distraction. Ironically, as I was putting the finishing touches on this chapter, he went to meet his God. For what my opinion is worth, I don't think he got the warm reception he was expecting. But then again, maybe he got a *really* warm reception. The man just had a mean, condescending spirit about him, but I honestly hope he made it.

How should the church respond to this issue? It's hard to say how I would feel if I had to confess a neon sin like homosexuality to my pastor. But I think some principal always needs to precede our policy. As with the old saying, you can draw more flies with honey than with vinegar. Before I tell someone he needs to walk away from his whole way of life, I need to at least hear his story.

I need to sympathize with the loneliness and the rejection of living in a world that was designed and constructed for straight people.

I need to understand what's it like to have a parent turn his or her back on someone. I need to listen to that person's struggle and understand why he is coming to me. And when I have really listened with my heart, then we can talk about how that person going to change.

That's my bottom line. That's the man I want to be.

One last thing. In Romans 1, Paul makes a very clear distinction between natural and unnatural affection. Homosexuality is not natural affection; we all know that.

7

Did Jesus ever address the subject of homosexuality?

Yes he did, directly and indirectly. When Jesus spoke about the covenant of marriage, he always had a built in assumption that marriage was between a man and a woman.

> "Haven't you read," he replied, "that at the beginning **the Creator made them male and female**, and said, 'For this reason a **man** will leave his **father** and **mother** and be united to his **wife**, [not domestic partner] and the two will become one flesh'? So they are no longer two, but one flesh. (Matthew 19:4–6)

Right there, Jesus tells you what his biblical understanding of a marriage is: one man and one woman. And yes, only two people—Jesus never advocated polygamy. It says, united with his *wife*, not *wives*.

Even in church leadership, Paul had a built-in assumption that anyone who was aspiring to be a pastor was a straight up and down guy. When you look at 1 Timothy, chapter 3, Paul gives a list of qualifications for deacons, elders, and overseers. One of the top requirements is that he must be the "husband of one wife." There is an assumption built into the text: "One adult sexual partner of the opposite sex for life." That was Paul's idea of a marriage.

But did Jesus ever address the subject of homosexuality specifically?
Yes he did, directly and indirectly. First let's deal with the indirect reference.

Jesus never used a specific word, name, or title for many things, but he certainly addressed the issue. When Jesus addressed the question of divorce, adultery, and remarriage in Matthew 19:9, he said, "I tell you that anyone who divorces his wife, except for **sexual immorality**, and marries another woman commits adultery."

What verse 9 actually said in the original Greek was, "Anyone who divorces his wife, except for **porneia**" (sexual immorality). Porneia is what we get the word *pornography* from.

Two words in the New Testament are translated as adultery. Matthew uses both of them in Matthew 19:9. At the beginning of the verse, he uses the word *porneia*. And at the end of the verse, he uses the word *moichao*, which is the more specific word for adultery in the Greek language. Why does he do that?

What Jesus was saying by the use of the word *porneia* is that a man could leave his wife for any violation of their sexual covenant, not just adultery. The word *porneia* in the days of Jesus was an all-inclusive word that indicated any violation of the sexual covenant.

It would have included fornication; prostitution; incest; homosexuality; bestiality; pedophilia; fathering illegitimate children; and of course, adultery. This is the exact meaning Jesus wanted this word to convey. He wanted us to know that all violations of the sexual covenant between a man and a woman were sinful and damaging to their relationship. He shot buckshot instead of a slug! If you are going to say that Jesus never objected to homosexuality because he never used that one specific word, then you have to believe that he was okay with bestiality, pedophilia, incest, prostitution, fathering illegitimate children, and wife beating because he never specifically mentioned any of those behaviors either.

Remember, when Jesus addressed the issue of adultery, he raised the bar. Just to refresh our memories, the seventh commandment is, "Thou shalt not commit adultery" (Exodus 20:14).

He was referencing the seventh commandment when he said, "You have heard that it was said, 'You shall not commit adultery. But I tell you that anyone who **looks at a woman lustfully** has already committed adultery with her in his heart" (Matthew 5:27–28).

If you believe that Jesus did not have an opinion on homosexuality, then you have to believe that he *raised* the bar on the sin of adultery, but *lowered* the bar on homosexuality to zero. Does that sound logical to you?

Did Jesus ever make a specific statement for or against homosexual behavior? Yes he did!

In Revelation, chapter 22, Jesus appears to the apostle John in a vision on the island of Patmos and gives John a very clear list of things that will keep a man out of heaven.

> Blessed are those who wash their robes, that they may have the right to the tree of life and may go through the gates into the city. [Heaven] Outside are the **dogs**, [homosexuals] those who practice magic arts, the sexually immoral, the murderers, the idolaters and everyone who loves and practices falsehood. (Revelation 22:14–15)

What does Jesus mean by *dogs*? He is referencing an ancient metaphor in the Torah, where homosexuals are referred to as dogs.

"You shall not bring the **hire of a harlot** or the **wages of a dog** into the house of the Lord your God for any votive offering, for both of these are an abomination to the Lord your God." In Deuteronomy 23:18, the Torah refers to a male prostitute as a dog, customers included.

Jesus says there is a sign in heaven right at the city gate: "No Dogs Allowed." Yes, Jesus had an opinion on homosexuality. He said you would go to hell for it if you did not repent and walk away from that lifestyle.

> It was the same in the days of Lot. People were eating and drinking, buying and selling, planting and building. But the day Lot left **Sodom, fire and sulfur rained down from heaven and destroyed them all.** (Luke 17:28–29)

> If anyone will not welcome you or listen to your words, leave that home or town and shake the dust off your feet. Truly I tell you, it will be more bearable for **Sodom and Gomorrah** on the day of judgment than for that town. (Matthew 10:14–15).

> And you, Capernaum, will you be lifted to the heavens? No, you will go down to Hades. For if the miracles that were performed in you had been performed in **Sodom**, it would have remained to this day. But I tell you that it will be more bearable for **Sodom** on the day of judgment than for you. (Mathew 11:23–24)

Yes, Jesus had an opinion on homosexuality.

8

Did Jesus ever address the issue of how to deal with a pedophile or someone who has bizarre sexual urges?

Three different times in the gospel narratives Jesus seems to be connecting some dots, and an honest student of the Bible will always ask why. Remember that what I am about to say is just one man's opinion on any given day. Search the Scriptures to formulate your own conclusion on this.

If you are totally honest, you know that Jesus had an opinion on issues like this. Any Rabbi that was well versed in the law of Moses would have an opinion on this. This is a moral and spiritual issue that cuts as deep as anything, and we all have an opinion on this. The Roman Emperor Commodus had a harem of three hundred women and boys. Yes, this was a huge problem in the Roman empire, and Jesus did not ignore the reality of what he saw going on around him. He warned people.

On two different occasions, Jesus addressed the issue of improper sexual impulses. Both times he said it would be better to voluntarily cut off parts of your own body than to have your whole body cast into outer darkness on the day of judgment.

1. In Mark 9, he caught his disciples arguing about who was the greatest in the kingdom of heaven. So he asked them, "What are you arguing about?" They said nothing because they were embarrassed. Jesus, knowing their thoughts, settled the argument by taking a little child in his arms and saying, "Anyone who welcomes one of these little children in my name welcomes me" (v. 32).

The disciples tried to change the subject by telling him they had seen a man casting out evil spirits in his name. Jesus responded to the allegation, turning the conversation right back around to the original discussion.

> Whoever causes one of these **little ones** who believe to stumble, it would be better for him if, with a heavy millstone hung around his neck, he had been cast into the sea. **If your hand causes you to stumble, cut it off;** it is better for you to enter life crippled, than, having your two hands, to go into hell, into the unquenchable fire, where their worm does not die, and the fire is not quenched. **If your foot causes you to stumble, cut it off**; it is better for you to enter life lame, than, having your two feet, to be cast into hell, where their worm does not die, and the fire is not quenched. **If your eye causes you to stumble, throw it out**; it is better for you to enter the kingdom of God with one eye, than, having two eyes, to be cast into hell, (Mark 9:42–47)

Did you catch the implied lesson in all that? If any part of your body causes one of these *little ones* to stumble, it would be better to go through life maimed than to spend eternity in hell. In Mark 10 he talks about a proper physical relationship between a man and a woman and ends the discussion by taking little children in his arms and blessing them (v. 16). He keeps connecting those dots.

God Said What

2. In Matthew 19 you see a similar dialogue, where Jesus spends the first half of the chapter making his case that a proper sexual relationship is between a man and a woman. He finishes his lesson by laying his hands on little children and blessing them (see v. 14–15).

But in the middle of this dialogue, he makes a very interesting statement.

> Not all men can accept this statement, **but only those to whom it has been given**. [He's telling you this does not apply to everybody] For there are **eunuchs** who were born that way from their mother's womb; and there are **eunuchs** who were made **eunuchs** by men; and there are also **eunuchs who made themselves eunuchs for the sake of the kingdom of heaven.** He who is able to accept this let him accept it. (Matthew 19:11–12)

Now, let's be true to the text. This statement was in response to the original question, Is it better for a man not to marry?

We always assume that this command was directed toward men who were lusting after women. Well, is making yourself a eunuch always for the purpose of total concentration to God, or could a man make himself a eunuch because he's oddly interested in something else? Why would someone make himself a eunuch just because he was not interested in women? If I were not interested in women, castrating myself is the last thing I would do!

I think he's addressing a deeper impulse than the lack of desire to marry someone of the opposite sex. Remember, he had just told them that the only proper physical relationship was between a man and a woman.

So, he started out teaching on proper sexual boundaries for adults and finished with blessing small children. But in the middle, he dropped a theology lesson on getting castrated. Odd, I know, but what was his point?

47

Well, here is what I do know. He made it very clear that if you have uncontrollable sexual impulses to hurt children, you'd better do something about it for the sake of your eternal soul, even if that means castrating yourself.

I also want to emphasize that Jesus said, "Some men made themselves eunuchs for the sake of the kingdom of heaven." This was not a command to the church; it was advice to someone who was off kilter. It was self-application. *You wanna make it to heaven? This is what you need to do, because you're not getting into heaven doing that to a child.*

Jesus also said, "there are **eunuchs** who were made **eunuchs** by men" (Matthew 19:12). Could this have been a Jewish punishment for crossing inappropriate lines with a child? If it were, it would fit the context of his lesson.

I know the eunuch suggestion seems a little extreme, but for someone who has an urge to mess with small children, voluntary surgical castration seems like a small price to pay compared to eternity in hell! I would counsel that person to take whatever precautions necessary to neutralize that desire. And with the benefit of modern medicine, doctors can even do chemical injections to neutralize sex drive. A tough subject, I know, but Jesus brought it up, not me!

One last thing: God has a lot to say about how we treat the weakest and most vulnerable members of our society. God has a real soft spot in his heart for weak, defenseless people who have no capacity to fight back.

9

Why did God order the execution of anyone who cursed his mother and father?

> Anyone who curses their father or mother is to be put to death. Because they have cursed their father or mother, their blood will be on their own head. (Leviticus 20:9)

The word *curse* in Hebrew goes a lot deeper than name-calling. It also means to defame or to misrepresent someone's personal integrity. To destroy someone publically.

Let's take a journey back in time. Most people in the Middle East lived in small farming communities, usually up to a hundred people. The people in any given village knew everybody and were interconnected in some way socially, spiritually, and economically. They were dependent upon each another for economic survival (you buy my stuff, and I'll buy your stuff). Without that kind of local support, a man could never survive. And usually a man's whole life was lived five miles from where he was born.

Let's set the stage. The scene changes because an unfortunate family in town has a rebellious son. He terrorizes the entire village. He's out of control. This is what the Bible calls an *incorrigible son*. No one can restrain him; he's an embarrassment. He's a lazy drunkard and refuses to work. No one wants to hire him or work with him. He's the guy no one wants to identify with. He cannot be trusted because he's a thief. He's always looking for the next opportunity to take advantage of an innocent person.

He decides that it's time to leave, and he wants his portion of the inheritance from his father. But the father refuses to give it to him because he knows what he'll do with it. So the son devises a plan to get rid of his parents. Murder is too messy. Waiting until they die will take too long. But he has a thought. "Start a good rumor, lie about my parents, and tell the village elders my dad is a dirty old man and Mom just looks the other way." The son blames his current condition on what the father did to him. The lie sticks. *It all makes sense now.*

The rumor spreads like a cancer. As the parents walk through the market place, people look and whisper. The only thing they can do is leave quietly in the middle of the night with the clothes on their backs. "Whoever robs their father and drives out their mother is a child who brings shame and disgrace." (Proverbs 19:26)

According to Jewish law, the son inherits everything. Mission accomplished. Driven from their homeland, they are disgraced and will never get to see their family or friends again. And they are old, so they have to relocate far away so that no one will ever know their "tainted" past. How do you fight a lie like that? With tears in their eyes, they leave everything behind to a son who will soon squander their life's work. There is nothing they can do to reverse the process that the son set in motion. Their blasphemous son has ruined their life, and the only thing they can do is hire themselves out as servants, the very thing the son was too lazy to do.

God says *kill the man*. Stone him to death. Anyone that selfish and wicked deserves to die. And not just for what he did. Anyone who is that evil is an unpredictable threat to society. Those in the community are living in fear and looking over their shoulders.

He just can't be trusted. They can't even trust their kids around him. God says a man like that has sealed his own fate. Take him out and stone him. Now, having said this, it is an interesting fact that we never have a record of anyone in the Bible being stoned because he cursed his father or mother. Maybe this was a warning to every young man. "Don't let the Devil tempt your heart to go there; don't even think about it."

10

Did God say, If a man rapes a woman, he has to marry her?

> If a man finds a girl who is a virgin, who is not engaged, and seizes her and lies with her **and they are discovered**, then the man who lay with her shall give to the girl's father fifty shekels of silver, and she shall become his wife because he has violated her; he cannot divorce her all his days. (Deuteronomy 22:28–29)

Before we dive into the text, we have a serious translation problem here. There is no one single word in the Hebrew language that specifically identifies something as a rape. The word *rape* does not exist in the Hebrew language. The word *rape* in the Bible comes from two Hebrew words: *taphas* and *shakab*. The first word means *to lay hold of*. The second word means *to lie down with*.

This verse literally translates to, "If he takes hold of her and lies down with her." Nothing in the original Hebrew indicates this was a forced sexual encounter—just two bodies intertwined. The word *shakab* is also used in the Bible to identify someone who has committed adultery. Now let's look at the actual wordage used in this text.

Dan Ver Woert

The first thing in that statement that knocks me a little off center is at the end of verse 28. It does not say, "if she turns him in." It says, "and they are discovered." Does that phrase indicate a spark of mutual consent? In this historical context, an unmarried man and woman crossing the line of sexual intimacy could have been considered rape by Jewish standards. Because the man had all the social leverage in the relationship and the woman had none.

We would refer to this today as being taken advantage of. I suggest an element of mutual consent, because the Bible was written in a patriarchal society. There were a lot of abusive, controlling men, and God knew this. If a young woman had an abusive, controlling father, she was trapped and hopeless. Is it possible a few of God's laws provided a loophole for a young girl to get out of this kind of bondage? Let's see.

> "If a man **seduce**s a virgin who is not pledged to be married and sleeps with her, he must pay the bride-price, and she shall be his wife. **If her father absolutely refuses to give her to him,** he must still pay the bride-price for virgins." (Exodus 22:16–17)

Two things really hit me in that text.

1. "If a man **seduce**s her" (v. 16). I have two daughters, and I would never give one of them to a man who had raped her or coerced her into doing something she did not desire, and neither would you. Seduction implies mutual consent.
2. "If her father absolutely **refuses** to give her to him" (v. 17), Hypothetically, the young woman desperately wants to be out from under her father's control. The young couple meets behind the barn and agrees to say it was mutual consent. All he has to do is come up with the bride price. Fifty shekels of silver and it's a win-win situation. Would a smitten young woman with a

controlling father do that? You bet she would! Now, according to verse 17, her father could still refuse. But I think most dads; at that point, knowing they lost the battle would consent to the will of the daughter.

11

Why Did God command us to take our dead brother's spouse as a wife?

First of all, that's not really what it says.

> When brothers live together and one of them dies and has no son, the wife of the deceased shall not be married outside the family to **a strange man**. Her husband's brother shall go in to her and take her to himself as a wife and perform the duty of a husband's brother to her. It shall be that the firstborn whom she bears shall assume the name of his dead brother, so that his name will not be blotted out from Israel.
>
> But if the man does not desire to take his brother's wife, then his brother's wife shall go up to the gate to the elders and say, 'My husband's brother refuses to establish a name for his brother in Israel; he is not willing to perform the duty of a husband's brother to me.' Then the elders of his city shall summon him and speak to him. And if he persists and says, 'I do not desire to take her,' then his brother's wife shall come to him in the sight of the elders, and pull his sandal off his foot and spit in his face; and she shall declare, 'Thus it is done to the man who does

> not build up his brother's house.' In Israel his name shall be called, 'The house of him whose sandal is removed.' (Deuteronomy 25:5–10)

This is not advocating polygamy. This was all about protecting the woman from an evil society—a society that exploited women who did not have the covering of a husband or a father. A widow having no son to protect her was a death sentence.

God said, "the living brother was to perform the duty of a husband." This was not about sex. It was about providing her with a son to take care of her in her old age. It also says that the offspring of this relationship was to "assume the dead brother's name." This is what entitled her to her fair portion of her father-in-law's inheritance when he died. Yes, this law was about money and about protecting and providing for the woman socially and economically. This was God's primary concern.

In that culture four thousand years ago, she could not just walk down the street and get a job at Wal-Mart. It didn't work that way. Without the social covering of a husband, she was fair game for anyone who wanted to exploit her. This is why God says, "She shall not be married outside the family to a **strange man**." She is to stay within the protection of her own immediate family.

Once her life and identity had been molded into another family, to just shove her out the door was a death sentence. Because she had already been married, she was seen as damaged goods. This law kept her from having to sell herself to the highest bidder. It's an anti-prostitution law. Where did the sandal and the spitting come from? Tradition. Here is how the Bible records it.

> Now this was the **custom** in former times in Israel concerning the redemption and the exchange of land to **confirm any matter**: a man **removed his sandal and**

> **gave it to another**; and this was the manner of attestation in Israel. (Ruth 4:7)

Exchanging a sandal solidified a transaction between two parties—their version of a signature on the dotted line. The sandal sealed the deal. And spitting in someone's face is a universal sign of disdain, as we all know.

By a good spit in the face, she was saying, "You would rather throw me to the dogs than fulfill your duty to your own brother?" Is that how you would want my husband to treat your wife if the tables were turned? Would you want your wife to be forced to marry a strange man outside the family? What about the golden rule? To force your sister-in-law to marry a strange man—that was cruel. Example:

> The **wife** of a man from the company of the prophets cried out to Elisha, Your servant my husband is **dead**, and you know that he revered the Lord. But now his creditor is coming to, **take my two boys as his slaves.** (2 Kings 4:1)

If the brother or relative of the dead husband did not take her in and take care of her, she had only one option left: she'd have to sell her two boys as slaves. It was a cruel option.

God always makes sense doesn't he? The lesson is not that a man refused to have sex with this dead brother's wife but how passionate God was about preserving the dignity and livelihood of a widow.

12

Why did God condemn a man for not impregnating his dead brother's wife?

The story of Onan, the second born of Judah, was an odd tale of three shady brothers and a would-be daughter-in-law.

> At that time, Judah left his brothers and went down to stay with a man of Adullam named Hirah. There Judah met the daughter of a Canaanite man named Shua. He married her and made love to her; she became pregnant and gave birth to a son, who was named Er. She conceived again and gave birth to a son and named him **Onan**. She gave birth to still another son and named him Shelah. It was at Kezib that she gave birth to him.
>
> Judah got a wife for Er, his firstborn, and her name was Tamar. But Er, Judah's firstborn, was wicked in the Lord's sight; so the Lord put him to death. Then Judah said to Onan, "Sleep with your brother's wife and fulfill your duty to her as a brother-in-law to raise up offspring for your brother." But Onan knew that the child would not be his; so whenever he slept with his brother's wife, he spilled his semen on the ground to keep from providing offspring for his brother. What he did was wicked in the

Lord's sight; so the Lord put him to death also. Judah then said to his daughter-in-law Tamar, "Live as a widow in your father's household until my son Shelah grows up." For he thought, "He may die too, just like his brothers." So Tamar went to live in her father's household. (Genesis 38:1–11)

This is possibly the oddest story in the Bible. A guy gets 99 percent of the way there, and then … well, you get the idea. And God says he's dead!

So what was the violation of morality here? In short …

1. Onan shifted the responsibility of his brother's wife from himself back to her aged parents.
2. Onan denied her the privilege of ever having children of her own.
3. Onan refused to carry on his brother's name, which was everything in this culture.
4. Onan used a desperate woman in a desperate situation for cheap sexual gratification. He knew that he was the only real option she had and played that to his advantage.
5. Onan knew that his kids would have to share their inheritance with Tamar's children. Yes, the decision to not follow through on the process was primarily a selfish financial decision.

Let's go back to number one: Onan shifted the responsibility of his brother's wife from himself back to her aged parents.

Judah (the father in law) told Tamar to, "Go live as a widow in your father's household until my son Shelah grows up." Both men dodged their responsibility to take care of this woman and tried to buy some time until the little brother grew up, hoping the Tamar problem would just go away. It was not Tamar's fault that her first husband, Er, was a renegade who had met the wrath of the Almighty. When the second son would not fulfill his responsibilities to his older brother, Judah and his family should have shouldered some of the responsibility of taking care of Tamar, because they raised two morons.

They knew this, they denied it, and they sent her back home. Let's put everything in its proper historical perspective. This was about five hundred years before the law of Moses. There was no real moral template to follow. Genesis 38 is still in the patriarchal period of the Bible. Part of what the law of Moses did was to confirm things in the Jewish culture that were already done right.

Remember from our previous chapter that if a man died, his brother had to take his wife so she did not have to marry a strange man. This is a good example of that. By Onan not taking care of his brother's wife, the two adjoining families had to decide what to do with Tamar. Talk about an embarrassing situation! They made it very clear that they did not want Tamar around and sent her back home. How dehumanizing! This story is not about sex. It's about the ethical responsibility of taking care of a widow. We keep revisiting that truth don't we?

It's hard for us to understand, but in this culture, the man did not marry into the woman's family; the woman married into the man's family. At the wedding there was an unspoken code of ethics that if something ever happened to the son, the son's family would step in to take care of her. The sin of Onan was an attempt at sidestepping that responsibility. But remember what Tamar did to her father-in-law, Judah? She got even.

After Judah's wife died, he took a short trip to visit some friends who were shearing sheep. When Tamar was told that her father-in-law was passing by on the road, she took off her widow's clothes and put on something seductive. Then she put a veil over her face to conceal her true identity. Tamar knew the youngest brother, Shelah, had grown up, but Judah had failed to keep his promise. She was still a widow-in-waiting, and she was ready was strike!

When Judah saw her, he assumed she was a prostitute and made an offer. She counter offered with "What's in the deal for me?"

Answer: "A young goat."

Tamar said, "but I need a pledge that you're going to uphold your end of the deal." She knew he lacked integrity in everything he did.

"What do you want as a pledge?" asked Judah.

"Your seal, its cord, and the staff in your hand." In other words, Judah's identification.

He gave it to her, and the deal was done. They had their moment, and when he left, she took off her veil and put her widow's cloths back on. About three months later, Judah got the word that his daughter-in-law Tamar was guilty of prostitution and was pregnant.

Upholding his deplorable reputation, Judah said, "Bring her out and have her burned to death!" Do you see the hypocrisy in that? Don't hold me accountable for my sin, but when we catch a woman doing the same thing, it's death on demand.

This was a corrupt family from the top down. But as she was being brought out, she sent a message to Judah. "I am pregnant by the man who gave me this seal this cord and this staff." Gulp! Judah made an astonishing statement. "She is more righteous than I, since I wouldn't give her to my son Shelah." He admitted he threw her to the dogs. They just couldn't beat this poor lady up enough could they? But Tamar got sweet revenge.

The good news: When it came time to deliver, it was twin boys—Perez and Zerah. In the genealogy of the Messiah, Matthew 1:3 is a home run: "Judah the father of **Perez and Zerah**, whose mother was Tamar." All four of them are mentioned in the genealogy of the Messiah!

The final lesson from this story: Our God is a God of redemption!

13

Why did God strike a man dead for touching the ark of the covenant?

They set the ark of God on a new cart and brought it from the house of Abinadab, which was on the hill. **Uzzah** and Ahio, sons of Abinadab, were guiding the new cart. with the ark of God on it, and Ahio was walking in front of it. David and all Israel were celebrating with all their might before the Lord, with castanets, harps, lyres, timbrels, sistrums and cymbals.

When they came to the threshing floor of Nakon, **Uzzah** reached out and took hold of the ark of God, because the oxen stumbled. The Lord's anger burned against Uzzah because of his irreverent act; therefore God struck him down, and he died there beside the ark of God. (2 Samuel 6:3–7)

I remember the first time I read this I thought, "Wow! I didn't know God had mood swings!" What was it that inflamed his anger like this?

This is where you have to piece a few things together from the Bible. The story starts out in 1 Samuel 5, when the Philistines captured the ark from Israel and brought it into Dagon's Temple. Bad idea. First, God cursed the land with an infestation of rats, and then he inflicted the Philistines, young and old, with very painful tumors for doing this. And those tumors, the Septuagint translates as *tumors in the groin*. I don't even want to go there. Ouch!

The first big mistake was that the Philistines put the ark of the covenant into a cart and sent it back into the Israelite camp. Even though this was an attempt to appease the anger of Yahweh, it was a clear violation of how the ark was to be transported.

Numbers, chapter 4, gives very detailed instructions about how the ark was to be transported, and only the Levites were to transport it. Gold rings were mounted on all four corners, and golden rods were inserted through the rings so the ark could be carried on the shoulders of Levites.

This was a symbol of how God carried them through the wilderness for forty years and how his presence never left them. He was their provider, savior, and deliverer. His presence went before them—a cloud of glory during the day and a pillar of fire by night.

But what made God so angry? Was it really the unauthorized touch, or was there something deeper? The answer is buried in one little detail in the text.

After Israel got the ark back, they brought it to the house of Abinadab and his two sons, Uzzah and Ahio. Uzzah is mentioned first because he was the oldest son, the obvious heir to his father's spiritual dynasty and next in line to be the spiritual priest of his family. Abinadab must have been a very important priest for them to have left the ark in his care. So Uzzah's dad was a spiritual and community leader. A big shot.

Do you see the seeds of pride being sown in a young man's mind? The devil whispers into his ear. "You are going to be really big some day, Uzzah, just like your dad. You are above the law. You can do nothing wrong. You sat by the ark every day as people passed through your home. They all wanted to see this strange and glorious sight. What a privileged family you have, that the great I AM selected you and your family as the chosen ones. Go ahead and take a sense of ownership. Bend the rules a little. You will never be held to the same standard as a common man."

So he reached out and touched the ark. Boom! Do you think that maybe, deep in his heart, he had cultivated a sense of entitlement? "The ark belongs to me; it's my property. I'm coming through. Everybody else get away. It's mine."

"As man looks at the outer appearance, God looks at the heart." And God did not like what he saw.

The priests underwent a lengthy and detailed ceremonial cleansing before they were allowed to go into the Holy of Holies or touch the ark. Did Uzzah take those precautions? The text certainly does not indicate that he did. I think he had lost his sense of reverence for God's presence. The sacred had become common to him, and it would cost him his life. Remember, when they touched the ark, they touched the very presence of God. Can any man take ownership of the presence of God? No.

A simple lesson here: *don't ever make God mad*. I don't feel like God has ever asked me for much in comparison to what he has done for me. So, when he does ask for something, that's all the more reason I do my best to comply right down to the letter. Anything less takes advantage of his grace and mercy over my life.

But can a man reach out and touch the presence of God today? Yes! "But we have this treasure in earthen vessels, that the excellency of the power may be of God, and not of us" (2 Corinthians 4:7).

The Blood of Jesus did all of that for us. He is our ceremonial cleansing. He is our altar. He is our entrance into the Holy of Holies. Thank you, Jesus!

14

Is suicide the unpardonable sin?

I have heard many well-intentioned preachers berate their congregation with the promise of eternal damnation. "Any man who takes his own life is dammed to an eternal hell!"

Before we speculate on what we don't know, let's start with what we do know. The Bible never connects the idea of suicide with the unpardonable sin, and it never addresses the subject of mental illness and how it plays into the role of suicidal tendencies. The Bible never attempts to address all of the social, spiritual, economic, and underlying psychological issues that would drive someone to commit suicide.

But we do have references in the Bible of people going insane like Nebuchadnezzar did in Daniel, chapter 4. According to the Gospel writers, some insane people were demonically possessed and controlled, like the Gadarene demoniac in Luke, chapter 8. After Jesus got a legion of evil spirits out of him, he sat there "clothed and in his **right mind**."

This one statement indicates his real problem was spiritual, not psychological. But without meeting someone, that's a hard to call to make.

So, when a man commits suicide, is it a psychological breakdown or is it a spiritual breakdown? I'm sure it's a whole lot of both.

One of the darkest spots in American history.

It is well documented that women on African slave ships, unable to cope with the trauma of being exploited by the slave captains, would grab their babies and jump overboard only to be eaten by sharks that followed the ship. Are they in hell? No. But the men who drove them there sure are. Yes, I believe in hell.

Let me take a quick pastoral excursion here. The issues I am very vocal about are the same issues that God is very vocal about. The issues that God is rarely vocal about, I maintain a reserved opinion on. This is one of those issues, because the Bible does not say exactly what happens to a person who commits suicide.

However, God said, "Thou shalt not murder." And that means even killing yourself. I would hate to stand before God having just taken my own life. Not the best introduction.

We're going to look at three men in the Bible who committed suicide. And I'm going to give you one "Yes, I think he's in hell," one "I don't really know where he went," and one "I'm sure he's in heaven."

1. Judas Iscariot:

The story of Judas is pretty straightforward. Judas gets picked to be one of the twelve. He even has an official title: treasurer. He's in charge of the money purse. But his heart was never right. Jesus said, "I have chosen you the twelve and yet one of you is a devil?" (John 6:70).

I know this raises a lot of questions: Did Jesus pick a devil? Or did Judas become a devil? Probably a little bit of both. But, Jesus saw it coming. He knew what was brewing inside of Judas's heart. Finally, the moment came when Judas had to make a decision. "It's him or me; one of us has to go."

Just so we don't forget …

Judas instigated the kiss of betrayal. Talk about a good friend / bad friend story! He arranged a signal. "The one I kiss is the one you want. Hail, Rabbi!" It's the kiss of death.

Jesus said, "Friend, do what you have come for" (Matthew 26:49). Let's get some perspective here. Judas would have thrown his own grandma to the dogs to save himself. That's just the kind of man he was.

Judas was a thief. "As keeper of the moneybag, he used to help himself to what was put into it" (John 12:6). A man who will lie about how he handles the church's money will lie about anything. Jesus entrusted him with taking care of the ministry's resources, and Judas betrayed that trust.

Judas was two-faced. Remember the woman in John 12 with the expensive jar of perfume? She anointed the feet of Jesus before his crucifixion, and when Judas saw what she had done, he threw a fit and said, "Why was this perfume not sold for three hundred denarii and the money given to the poor?" Sounds like a really spiritual response doesn't it?

But here's the kicker, "He [Judas] did not say this because he cared about the poor, but because he was a thief" (John 12:6). False compassion. Judas was the kind of man who would lie about having an orphanage just to scam a dollar.

Judas was being driven by the powers of darkness. Judas set the stage; the mob showed up wielding clubs and swords. He sold Jesus to the crowd for thirty pieces of silver. And when Judas took the money, "Satan entered Judas" (Luke 22:3). How does a man go to heaven with Satan in his heart? He doesn't.

Judas was a traitor. Jesus was nothing but good to Judas. He gave him the chance of a lifetime. Jesus said, "Many prophets and righteous people longed to see what you see but did not see it" (Matthew 13:17). But Judas threw it all to the wind.

Judas was a mess. How does a thief and a two-faced backstabber who's full of the Devil hear the words *well done* when he stands before God? He doesn't. Jesus said in Matthew 26, "The Son of Man will go just as it is written of him, but woe to that man by whom the Son of Man is betrayed! It would have been better for that man if he had **not been born**." *Better to have not been born?* In heaven? I don't think so.

Something grabbed Judas deep down on the inside, but it wasn't genuine remorse. It was the remorse of blowing the opportunity of a lifetime. It was being sorry he got caught. He tried to undo the rotten deal, but the process he set in motion had too much momentum behind it. All sins are forgivable, but not all sins are undoable. The story of Judas proves that.

In 2 Corinthians 7:10, Paul draws a contrast between two different kinds of remorse. "**Godly sorrow** brings repentance that leads to **salvation** and leaves no **regret**, but **worldly sorrow** brings **death**."

The difference between godly and worldly sorrow is that godly sorrow is being truly sorry that your sins have dishonored God. Worldly sorrow is being sorry that you got caught.

What do you see in the life of Judas? Do you see repentance that led to salvation or to death?

The most common Greek word for repent is *metanoia*, which means *to have a change of mind*. *Meta* is Greek for change. *Noia* is Greek for mind. I changed my mind.

The Bible says that "Judas was seized with remorse" (Matthew 27:3). The Greek word for remorse is *metamelomai*, and it should be translated as *Judas was sorry he got caught.*

So, Judas threw the bag of money into the potter's field, and how did he deal with his guilt and his shame? "Judas went and hung himself"

(Matthew 27:5). Suicide is not a logical response to true repentance, but it is a logical response to worldly remorse.

Where did Judas go when he died? We have three solid clues.

1. Only Judas and the antichrist are referred to in the Bible as the "son of perdition" (John 17:12 and 2 Thessalonians 2:3). The word *perdition* means, *the destruction of the soul*—a state of eternal damnation, where the unrepentant soul goes when it dies.
2. In Acts 1:24, the apostles cast lots to select another apostle to fill Judas's lot. Peter prayed and said, "Show us which of these two you have chosen to take over this apostolic ministry, which Judas left to go where he belongs."

"Which Judas left to go where he belongs." To me, that's a reference to hell.

3. In John 17:12, in the priestly prayer of Jesus, we see this:

> While I was with them, I protected them and kept them safe by that name you gave me. None has been lost except the one **doomed to destruction** so that Scripture would be fulfilled.

Does that sound like a free ticket to heaven?

Judas did not go to hell for committing suicide. He went to hell for the same reason anybody goes to hell: for saying no to God and not accepting his forgiveness for sins.

2. The suicide of King Saul

The war between the Israelites and the Philistines was raging hot, and Saul's three sons had already fallen in battle. Several Philistine archers had critically wounded Saul, who had been "plunked" by more than one arrow. "They wounded him critically" (1 Samuel 31:3).

Saul had lost the protection of the Holy Spirit, and his time was over. Saul said to his armor bearer, "take your sword and kill me, or they will take me and abuse me." Saul knew he only had two choices: either end his life or be tortured by a band of Philistine soldiers. His armor bearer refused, saying, "He could not raise his hand against the Lords anointed." So, Saul put the butt end of his spear into the ground and fell on it. When his armor bearer saw that Saul was dead, he fell on his own sword too.

Some would insist that Saul took the coward's way out. That's an easy thing to accuse someone of until you are standing in his shoes. Life as Saul had always known it was over. His three sons were dead, and if he lost this battle, he would have nothing left to go home to.

Even if the Philistines had let him live, they would have made him a slave, taunted his family, and stripped him of his throne. An Israelite king one day and a Philistine slave the next. Trust me, he had thought this through. A quick death or slow death? A humiliating death or a noble death? All of a sudden, that decision does not seem so cowardly.

When the Philistines came to strip the dead. They cut off Saul's head, they stripped off his armor, and they fastened his body to the wall at Beth Shan.

It's hard to say what went through his mind in those last minutes. Regrets, I'm sure. But does the Bible say he's in hell? I hope not, because under those circumstances, I would have done the same thing.

The hardest thing for a preacher to do is a funeral service for someone who was "riding the fence" in his Christian faith.

Is Pastor Dan going to preach this guy into heaven or hell? I tell people my policy at a funeral is to preach to the living. This message is for them.

But if people ask me privately where I think he is, I say he's in the hands of God. Whether he is in the hands of God's judgment or the hands of God's saving grace is for God to decide. In the words of Abraham: "Will not the Judge of the whole world do what is right?" (Genesis 18:25). Where did Saul go when he died? Heaven, I hope.

3. The suicide of Samson

I bet you never thought of Samson as a guy who committed suicide. The story of Samson's death is in Judges 16.

He fell in love with a woman named Delilah. The Philistines rulers cornered her privately and propositioned her. "If you can figure out the secret of his strength, each one of us will give you eleven hundred shekels of silver." This was back when women had no rights and no disposable income, so this was a major temptation, to say the least.

He lied to her three times about where his strength came from, and she was really frustrated about the whole thing. She prodded him and picked at him for so long he eventually gave in. "It's the hair honey; don't cut the hair." She put him to sleep on her lap and called for the local barber to come in.

And then the test: "Samson, the Philistines are upon you!" He was clueless. Then one of the saddest statements in the Bible says, "But he did not know that the spirit of the Lord had left him."

How does a man lose the indwelling of the Holy Spirit and not know it? I guess the power of sin chipped away at his heart so slowly and the change in his soul was so subtle that when he finally lost it all, it was not even noticeable. Ouch! The story gets worse: The Philistines bound him with bronze shackles and gouged out his eyes. They put him to grinding grain like an animal in a Philistine prison camp. But in time his hair started to grow again.

Party time. The Philistine rulers all got together and made a sacrifice to their god, Dagon, during a drunken wine fest. "Our god has delivered Samson, our enemy, into our hands."

Everybody shouted, "Bring out Samson to entertain us." But they made a huge mistake. They forgot about the hair. They stood him right next to the two pillars that held the temple roof in place.

He said to his servant, "Put me right in the middle of the two pillars so I can lean against them and rest for a minute." The temple was full, and three thousand men and women were on the roof. Samson prayed a simple prayer: "Let my strength come back to me one last time. And let me revenge these Philistines one last time for what they did to my eyes."

Putting one hand on each pillar, he uttered, "Let me die with the Philistines!" The ceiling started to shake, and it was too late. The building collapsed in on itself, and Samson killed more people that day than he had in his entire lifetime. But did you catch his last statement? "Let me die with these Philistines."

Some would argue that this was a martyr's death. I don't see that.

A true martyr is killed for not backing down on his or her personal convictions. I don't see Samson having a whole lot of conviction in his life. Sleeping with prostitutes, and so on.

I see a man who God used to protect his chosen people—a political Rambo. It was Samson's choice to die that day, and he did. They did not bring him into Dagon's temple to kill him, "to make sport of him." He took his own life.

So put down the bottle of 409, and stop trying to sanitize the text. It was a suicide. But it was a justifiable suicide in the eyes of God. If you listen to his last prayer with your heart, this becomes obvious. "Let the anointing and the power of the Holy Spirit flow through me one last time and let me fulfill my God appointed destiny, abolishing the enemies of God."

Samson gave it a big heave-ho and fulfilled his destiny.

How did they record that in the *Philistine Daily Gazette*?

Old, Crippled Blind Man Anointed One Last Time—Philistines Lose Big Time!

Where did Samson go when he died, heaven or hell? Here's my hope for Samson.

"I do not have time to tell about Gideon, Barak, **Samson** and Jephthah, about David and Samuel and the prophets, who through faith conquered kingdoms, administered justice, **and gained what was promised**" (Hebrews 11:32–33).

Samson is listed with a bunch of godly, faithful men and prophets who, through faith, fulfilled their God-given destiny "and **gained** what was promised." I find it hard to believe that a man who is listed in God's Hall of Fame did not make it to heaven. I believe Samson did make it to heaven. Just like the thief on the cross, who had a serious change of heart at the last minute. "Lord remember me when you come into your kingdom. And Jesus said, today you will be with me in paradise" (Luke 23:43).

One of the many lessons we learn from Samson is that taking our own life is not the unpardonable sin.

15

Would Jesus have supported the death penalty?

He did. When Jesus hung on that cross, by his own admission, he could have called twelve legions of angels to come and rescue him. A roman legion was six thousand men. So, twelve legions of angels is 72,000 angels. That was a lot of help at his disposal! (See Matthew 26:53.)

If he could have done that for himself, couldn't he have done that for those two thieves hanging there with him? Yes, but he didn't. He let them hang. The one thief even admitted, "we are getting what we deserve."

And Jesus did not respond by saying, "No, you're getting over-punished; no one deserves the death penalty for any reason." He let them hang.

If Jesus was 100 percent opposed to the death penalty, he missed a great opportunity to use his spiritual leverage to get these men out of this situation!

These men had been caught stealing another man's livelihood with no replacement insurance. Probably a lifetime of labor and sacrifice was gone in an instant. There were eighteen sins in the Old Testament that carried the death penalty, so yes, God believes in the death penalty.

It should also be noted that if the creator of a law wants to suspend, eliminate, or alter a law at any given time, he has the authority to do that. He is God, right? In John, chapter 8, there was a woman who was supposedly caught in the act of adultery.

The teachers of the law and the Pharisees tried to use the leverage of the Torah to get a death sentence, but Jesus did the unthinkable.

"Let he who is amongst you without sin, cast the first stone." He not only called their bluff but also recognized that adultery was a sin between two consenting individuals. And it was Jesus who said, "The son of man is Lord over the Sabbath." That it's okay to pull an ox out of a mud pit on the Sabbath. God can change or suspend any law he wants to.

Jesus and the apostles were all under Roman law. Paul tells us in Romans 13:4, "that He does not bear the **sword** for nothing, because they are God's servants, agents of wrath to bring punishment on the wrongdoer." What did a Roman soldier use his sword for, opening a can of tuna at lunchtime?

To say that God did away with capital punishment in the New Testament is to deny the facts. God killed Ananias and Sapphira in Acts 5 for lying to the Holy Spirit. But the two thieves on the cross? I do not know what these two men stole or whose life they terrorized. But obviously the nature of the crime demanded a death sentence. Maybe it was multiple offenses; it's hard to say.

In Acts 12, King Herod addressed a crowd of people, wearing his royal robe and sitting on his royal throne. They all shouted, "This is the voice of a god, not of a man." It says, "Immediately, because Herod did not give praise to God, an angel of the Lord struck him down, and he was eaten by worms and died."

Yes, even in the New Testament dispensation of grace, God still has a breaking point.

God Said What

Some have tried to discredit the biblical principal of stoning as a form of torture. God has never advocated torture. Stoning someone was God's way of giving a community permanent closure on a man who had violated and terrorized numerous people. "We finally caught the guy, and he's gone forever. Now, everybody, go home and sleep in peace."

Many times the victims were too intimidated to speak out. The predator usually played the retaliation card. "I'll get your mom and dad next!"

God knew the whole community needed a permanent closure on this man's existence. God said, "Let the elders of the community stone him" (see Deuteronomy 21).

Remember the name Ariel Castro? The monster that locked three young ladies in his house for ten years and violated them repeatedly, beat them, and rarely fed them? If I were running the country, he would have gotten one last chance to talk to the preacher, and then I would have hung him in the pubic square. Yes, I said that. And I'm sure you know he hung himself literally.

Capital punishment is a penalty for what someone did. But it does have a purging effect on society. It keeps dangerous people off the streets who can never be trusted. And it also sends a message to the predators of our society that they will not exploit our women and children like this and get away with it. It's a fear tactic. It's a deterrent. In ministry terminology, Ariel Castro "crossed the lines of irreversible integrity." We can never turn our backs on him again, and to stick him in a prison cell for life and send the taxpayers the bill is an insult. God never asked us to go there. God gave his blessing on removing the burden of these people from society. Ariel Castro forfeited all of his rights as a human being, and he deserved to die. And one of those three young ladies should have been given the chance to pull the lever. Remember, God condoned public stoning's for certain sins! "Anyone who kidnaps someone is to be put to death, whether the victim has been sold or is still in the kidnapper's possession." (Exodus 21:16)

The curse of a lousy legal system: Delayed justice is the violation of a biblical principal. What if I told you that every time one of my kids got in trouble I wrote it down on a calendar? Then at the end of the year, I brought him in, confronted him, and decided what his punishment was going to be. That sounds really ridiculous doesn't it?

That's how God feels when we let prisoners sit on death row for seventeen years and then make the decision to execute them. Delayed justice is the violation of a biblical principal. But the evidence has to be undisputable. This is why God's law demanded the testimony of two or three witnesses for someone to be executed. They were never allowed to execute someone on the basis of one witness or on the basis of hearsay. It had to be two or, preferably, three eyewitnesses (see Deuteronomy 17:6).

Yes, Jesus supported the death penalty.

16

Is it permissible for a woman to speak in church?

Facebook posting: "And God promised men that good and obedient wives would be found in all corners of the earth. Then He made the earth round … and He laughed and laughed and laughed!"

The question of unlimited submission? Two passages in the New Testament seem to limit the role of women in church leadership.

> Women should remain silent in the churches. **They are not allowed to speak**, but must be in submission, **as the Law says**. If they want to inquire about something, they should ask their own husbands at home; for it is **disgraceful** for a woman to speak in the church. (1 Corinthians 14:34–35)

> A woman should learn in quietness and full submission. I do not permit a woman to teach or to **assume authority** over a man; she must be quiet. (1 Timothy 2:11–12)

These two verses have been responsible for splitting churches and denominations for centuries. I'll use a true story as a backdrop.

Dan Ver Woert

I remember hearing a story about Anne Graham Lotz, the second child of Billy Graham. She was asked to address a large crowd at a multidenominational pastor's convention. When she stood up to preach, about half of the eight hundred men at the conference stood up, turned their chairs around, and sat down with their backs turned toward her just to make a point. No woman is going to preach to us!

How do I, as a pastor, reconcile a woman speaking in a public assembly with Paul's statements to the Corinthian church? Let's break it down one statement at a time.

"They are not allowed to speak, but must be in submission, **as the Law says**" (1 Corinthians 14:34b).

"As the Law says." What law? The only biblical law Paul could be referring to is the law of Moses, the Torah. And the law of Moses does not say that women were not allowed to speak in the local synagogue. There is not one reference in the Old Testament saying that a woman was not allowed to speak in a synagogue.

Was this a cultural law or some type of a Jewish elder law? I honestly don't know. But I do know he was not referring to a biblical law. Was this a command just for the Corinthian Church at that moment, or should that statement be a universal truth for all time and eternity?

Let's go back in time to a Jewish synagogue on a Sunday morning to recreate a Jewish worship experience in the first century. Men sat in the front of the church, and women sat in the back. Sometimes a veil separated them. I called a Jewish synagogue in Des Moines, Iowa, and asked, "How do you run a Jewish worship service?" The secretary told me that the synagogue is sectioned off down the middle.

If you were to visit, you would be taken to one side of the church and your wife to the other side, because men and women do not sit together in church. Right or wrong, in some Jewish worship services, they still do this today.

Part of what was going on is that the women were sitting in the back of the church behind the veil, blurting out questions, and being disruptive. This is why we see the statement, "If they have any questions, Wait and ask your husband when you get home" (1 Corinthians 14:35). Don't disrupt the service.

In the first century, men were educated and women were not. Boys went to school to learn the Torah, with hopes of becoming a Rabbi. But girls were trained for motherhood and domestic chores. Women were uneducated and asking entry-level questions that were taking up too much time to answer. In that culture women were not allowed to teach men, and a man would have never accepted a woman's instruction.

Women like Joyce Meyer and Beth Moore would have been silenced. Women were allowed to teach their own kids at home but never publicly. The good news is that Christianity changed all that. It liberated women back to their rightful place of influence in society.

Socially, when Paul wrote this, a women's liberation movement was going on in the city of Corinth. These women had shaved heads and were walking down the streets of Corinth bare-chested with spears in their hands. They shouted obscenities at men to let them know that they were not going to be treated as inferiors anymore. And this women's liberation movement contributed to the disorder in public worship. When you understand all this, you begin to see that Paul was not only trying to straighten out a church theologically but also a community as well.

This is where it all comes together.

"They are not allowed to **speak**" (1 Corinthians 14:34b) The Greek language, like most languages, usually has two or more words for everything.

In English we have several different words for *speak*: talk, converse, dialogue, discourse, communicate, interact, chatter, mumble, ramble. Then we have euphemisms like shooting the breeze, running your mouth off, blowing smoke, gibberish, and so on.

Greek is a lot like that. It is a much more descriptive language than most. Usually the words sound similar, but the nuances make a huge difference. Several Greek words can be translated *to speak* or *to talk*. But we're going to look at the two most common words: *Legeo* and *Lelao*.

Legeo: To speak the way you would speak to your neighbor, in a normal conversational tone.

Laleo: To chatter, to rattle on incessantly, to distort the truth.

On the day of Pentecost, when the Holy Sprit was poured out, the Bible says, "And they all began to "**Laleo**" in other tongues" (Acts 2:4). Meaning they began to chatter and ramble in such a way that no one could understand what was being said.

There was so much confusion in the upper room, the people who were there said, "These people are drunk, they have had to much wine!" But that's not what happened.

Paul actually says, "I forbid a woman to **Laleo**" (to chatter, to ramble, to disrupt the service from the back row, to distort the truth).

He does not say, "I forbid a woman to **Legeo**" (to speak in a normal conventional tone of voice). Is the fog starting to lift?

If a woman were not allowed to speak in church, how would she sing, pray, or worship? If women are not supposed to speak in church, why does Paul, just three chapters prior to this, spell out the proper attire for a woman to wear if she is going to pray or prophesy in church? Remember he tells her to cover her head (see 1 Corinthians 11:5).

Okay, let's deal with that since we're there. "But every woman who prays or prophesies with her head uncovered dishonors her head—it is the same as having her head shaved" (1 Corinthians 11:5).

My New Testament history professor at North Central University was a woman who did her doctoral dissertation in female prophets. She told us that the temple prostitutes in the city of Corinth would shave their heads as a sign of rebellion. Some of them would even yank the hair out of their heads and let the blood dry, just to look perverted and different.

Another professor told me concerning this verse that there was just an erotic mysticism about making love to a woman who had no hair. Odd, I know.

According to church historians, several of these women came into the church at Corinth and found the Messiah. Paul was telling them:

"Until your hair grows back out, put something over your head so you are not identified as an ex-temple prostitute." That is, don't be a distraction to the men. Back to my original point: can a woman speak in church?

"Give my greetings to the brothers at Laodicea, and to **Nympha** and the church in **her** home" (Colossians 4:15). How does a woman have a church in her home if she cannot speak?

In Romans 16:1 Phoebe is mentioned as a deaconess. How does a woman function as a deaconess if she cannot speak?

One of the most interesting things about the church in Philadelphia (Revelation 3) is that between the year 100 and 160 BC, a prophetess, Ammia, led it. She was recognized by all the early church fathers as being a true prophetess. So, how do you lead a church prophetically if you cannot speak?

How was she thrust into this position of leadership? I'm sure that there was a prophetic word spoken over her, and then there was a prophetic sense of confirmation in the local body that she was a prophetess.

Now let's deal with the second verse. "A woman should learn in quietness and full submission. I do not permit a woman to teach or **to usurp authority** over a man; she must be quiet" (1 Timothy 2:11–12).

To usurp authority over comes from a Greek word, *authentein*, used one time in the Bible. There are no other textual comparisons. So, we have to read "extra scriptural literature" to see how secular texts use this same word or phrase.

It was used in the first century to indicate murdering someone with a sword. An *authentes* was a murderer. *Authentein* is also connected with several suicides or masterminding a plot to overthrow someone with severe violence, which is how it's used in Greek literature.

It is used the same way the Bible translated it. To usurp authority over someone, to assume authority that you do not have. A Jezebel spirit. It does not forbid a woman to teach, but commands her to teach within a certain context. She is to be under the covering of her husband or the elders of a local church.

There are certain places the bible commands women too teach.

> Likewise, teach the **older women** to be reverent in the way they live, not to be slanderers or addicted to much wine, but to **teach** what is good. Then they can **teach** the

younger women to love their husbands and children, to be self-controlled and pure, to be busy at home, to be kind, and to be subject to their husbands, so that no one will malign the word of God. (Titus 2:3–5)

According to Paul, who is supposed to be in charge of teaching the young women in the church? The pastor? No, the older women. I don't have a lot to say to young mothers, but my wife sure does. Do you think that a bunch of men should be teaching young women how to be keepers at home? They are the ones who keep the house in order, so you want men teaching a class on that? Remember, the Bible says, "to avoid an appearance of evil." Real men have no desire to deal with these kinds of things; that's not our department.

John MacArthur says, "There is not one indication in the New Testament of a woman ever assuming a teaching role in the church." He's dead wrong! What about Anna, who prophesied over the baby Jesus in the temple? What about Phillip the Evangelist, who had four virgin daughters who all prophesied? (See Acts 21:9.) How does a woman prophesy and not offer instruction?

A New Testament example: Think about the order of these names: Adam and Eve, Abraham and Sarah, Isaac and Rebekah, Jacob and Leah. The man's name is always mentioned first. We still do this today. People always refer to my wife and me as Dan and Annette.

Aquila and Priscilla are mentioned six times in the New Testament. Three of those times, Priscilla's name is first: Priscilla and Aquila. They are never mentioned separately but always as a couple. They were an obvious ministry team.

In a Jewish or Roman culture, it was uncommon to switch the order of gender and mention the woman first. We know that Priscilla was involved in teaching the Word of God under the covering of her husband. "When

Aquila and **Priscilla** heard him, [Apollos] "**they**" took him aside and explained to him the way of God more accurately" (Acts 18:24–26). This was a team effort to help this man in his ministry. *They!*

Some denominations do not ordain women for pastoral ministry, but they do commission them to do full-time missionary work. Okay, so you can teach in an overseas mission, lead a Bible college, plant a church on foreign soil, travel, and speak in churches to raise a budget or testify to what God is doing in your ministry.

But you cannot teach from the pulpit on a Sunday morning? Yeah, that makes perfect sense.

The problem with being a Pharisee is you are always inconsistent. In the words of Jesus, "You strain out a gnat and swallow a camel." I have counted the pictures of missionaries on the back walls of many churches, and half of the ones they support on a monthly basis are single women. Go figure.

Priscilla was a true coequal with her husband in pastoral ministry. The first-century church and the apostles recognized this and tried to communicate this. I hope this settles the issue for you once and for all. Arise, Deborah!

Conclusion

Where do we go from here?

I'm going to switch gears right now, make my last point, and then give you an official good-bye.

We could cover other stories in the Bible. Lots of them. But I think we all get the point. Sometimes life doesn't make sense, and God steps into the picture to make sense out of the chaos we create. There are things God does, things that God allows, and bad situations we get ourselves into. Let's not blame God for the holes we dig.

I know this has been a somber journey through the Bible, so let's end on a good note.

The real lesson I want you to take from this book is this: no matter how corrupt or how vile mankind ever became, God never gave up on us. And he's not giving up on you. Having this book in your hand right now is living proof that you're a God chaser.

You wanted more of God in your life, and the time you spent walking through this book is proof of that. You have taken the time to know God better, and I hope at the end of this journey, we will all know each other better.

I don't think conflict between people and nations has as much to do with disagreement as it does with not understanding someone else's worldview. I hope I have challenged your worldview from a biblical perspective.

I hope you understand the worldview of the biblical narrative better, and I hope you feel an inch taller spiritually. I hope this book has changed how you see the character of God, the God of the Bible. The God who has revealed himself through his only begotten Son—the incarnate Son of God, Jesus Christ, Savior, baptizer, and soon-coming King.

Remember, Jesus told his disciples, "Rejoice not brethren that the demons submit to you in my name, rather rejoice that your names are written in the lamb's book of life." I hope to see you there when the names are read, and I hope our paths cross someday.

Pastor Dan Ver Woert

A special thanks to Pastors Aaron Gunsaulus and Josh Havens and for being my theological editors on this book. I could not have done it without your help. And to my old camp counselor Allan Ruter who gave me my first dictionary and inspired me to embrace the power of words.